# C O N T E N T S

CAROL CREGG  Derelict                                    11

DANIEL PEARSON  Frosty's Donuts                          19

GILLIAN FYFFE  Dilemmas of a Courtesan                   31

VICTORIA QUINN  An Interview with Will MacLean           41

FREYA REINSCH  Domestic                                  45

EMMA PARFITT  How the Herring Became a Kipper            61

LUKE HEELEY  The Splinter
             Two Poems                                   67

BARBARA FERGUSON  The Legend of the Vendors              77

HELEN STEPHEN  Sugar High                                85

HEATHER MURRAY  Five Poems                               92

DAWN BAUMGARTEN  Operator                                99

VICTORIA QUINN  Baba Yaga's Daughter
                Two Poems                                111

CHRISTIAN McLEAN  Koi                                    117

RACHEL HOLLON  A Local Habitation
               Two Poems                                 127

TRAVIS SENTELL  Playground                               135

AMY WOOLFORD  Wednesday                                  145

MARK LANGWITH  The Church Roof
               Two Poems                                 151

# SCORES

Published by Castle House Books 2002

Castle House Books, School of English
University of St Andrews, St Andrews, Fife KY16 9AL

Printed in Scotland by Woods of Perth
Design by Belstane

ISBN 0-9535963-2-X

# SCORES

WORK BY STUDENTS OF
THE M.LITT IN CREATIVE WRITING AT
THE UNIVERSITY OF ST ANDREWS

EDITED BY DOUGLAS DUNN
AND STUDENTS OF 2001-2002

CASTLE HOUSE BOOKS

# INTRODUCTION

SEVENTY-SIX STUDENTS have graduated from St Andrews's M.Litt course in Creative Writing since it was first offered in 1993. To begin with, the teaching Faculty consisted of myself, with some poetry classes given also by Robert Crawford, Professor of Modern Scottish Literature, and now also Head of School, a function which fell to my lot for too long. The course in the Novel was taught by a visiting novelist-in-residence, and we were fortunate in being able to appoint Alasdair Gray, Carl MacDougall, Alice Thompson, Brian McCabe, and Ron Butlin. Now, however, the course benefits from the presence of John Burnside, poet, short-story writer, novelist, ecologist, and who from September 2002 will be a full-time member of staff. Kathleen Jamie, poet, essayist, traveller, and much else, continues to teach on the poetry course in the first Semester as she has done since 1999. An additional two writers will be employed on a quarter-time basis from September 2002.

With such a strengthening of resources St Andrews can now offer an even better programme in writing than ever before, and at a time when many other universities in Scotland and throughout the British Isles are setting up programmes of their own.

Of those who have graduated from the course several have published. Matt Thorne's fiction has deservedly earned a prominent place in contemporary British writing. Sarah Bryant's *The Other Eden* appeared last year from TimesWarner in an electronic edition and in traditional hard copy. James Andrew has published a collection of poems while Andrew Zawacki's first collection appeared in 2001 from the University of Georgia Press. Sarah Hall's novel *Haweswater* came out with Faber and Faber early this summer. Henry Shukman's first collection of poems will appear from Jonathan Cape later this year and he has published short stories as well as much travel writing. Kate Scott's poems will be published by Peterloo Poets in 2003. Other students have gone into less expected lines of work. Bruce Jack, for example, from the first course, is now a winemaker (Flagstone Wines) in South Africa and his *Pinot noir* is as good a substitute for poetry as you could find. Holly Gregory fronts a children's TV programme in the U.S.A. Others have become teachers, or work in journalism, the media, publishing, bookselling, or are or have been Ph.D students at St Andrews or elsewhere.

Graduates from the course who've published more or less promptly are not always those I anticipated to step into print at the first time of asking. It's not exactly a case of "you never can tell"; it's more one of the pleasant surprise. Others, I'm sure, will break into print a little later on, while some will have decided that the perseverance of trying to become a writer is not for them. In any case, a year studying writing can never be a guarantee of eventual publication. What it should provide is a year of discovery and self-discovery, of reading, writing, and conversation, leading to a deeper understanding of literature, and, possibly, perhaps even probably, a sense of one's own talent. This year's large class of sixteen has been exemplary in the inquistiveness and conscientiousness of individual students. Each year, class by class, I've noticed how closely students bond and arrange their own additional workshops, the sheer extent to which they get to know each other, exchange ideas, recommend books and writers, and form not so much a university class as a community of young writers. St Andrews is good for that. It's a small and attractive town by the sea, redolent with a unique blend of antiquity, landscapes, seascapes, and the atmosphere of a twenty-first century Academy. As a small town students at all levels find themselves having to devise many of their own amenities and opportunities outside the academic timetable. In terms of classes and deadlines that timetable is demanding and offers more teaching contact hours than any other M.Litt in the Faculty of Arts. But I'm exhilarated by how students have extended it through their own efforts, simply through a dedication to their own work and to the subject of new literature.

This year, members of the class were particularly active in student drama, whether performing or writing. We also enjoyed a close association with Duncan of Jordanstone College of Art, of the University of Dundee, swapping visits and ideas with the MFA sudents there. Encouraged by Kevin Henderson, their course leader, we were able to mount a joint exhibition of art works and texts at Dundee Contemporary Arts in March 2002. Another highlight of the year was a visit by the poet and dramatist Stewart Conn in his role as the former drama producer for Radio Scotland, who gave an inspirational talk on exactly that subject. As the students were evidently taken by it, I thought it best to set one of the essay topics in the form of "Write a dramatization for radio of a nineteenth-century short story." What I didn't bargain for was that most of the students would opt for it. Nor did I expect the length of their adapations, and I certainly didn't anticipate their quality and ambition. Another optional 'essay' question in the poetry module, one which I always set, is "Write a history of blank verse in blank verse (or of rhyming couplets in rhyming couplets)" and that too has also had a heartening response.

Work represented here shows a wide range of backgrounds and approaches to writing, whether in prose or verse. None of it has been pasteurised or cloned by teachers although different ways of writing, alternative directions, have been pointed out, and authors indicated where teachers saw the likelihood of an affinity between a student's imagination or intentions and the work of a published or canonical author. Besides mundane corrections, suggestions, and advice, that forms an important part of teaching in a subject where a student is close to an apprentice but where the teacher would want to draw back from the status of master if only for the sake of avoiding the disagreeable experience of pontificating.

As Sloan Fellow in the School of English, James Robertson, novelist, short-story writer, poet, and publisher and editor of the small-press imprint Kettilonia, gave unstintingly of his time in the second Semester. His assistance in teaching tutorials and workshops was invaluable, as, indeed, was his help in second-marking essays and in particular those many radio adaptations of Gogol, Poe, Chekhov, and Leskov. Deborah Turner Harris, author of fantasy novels, who lives in St Andrews, provided tutorial assistance which was much appreciated by the students.

American spelling has been retained in work by American students.

This issue of *Scores* has once again been sponsored by the literary agency Peters, Fraser & Dunlop, to whom the School of English is indebted for its generous support of new writers.

Douglas Dunn

**Carol Cregg** is 22 and comes from Dublin. She attended Dublin City University, where she did a degree in Communications. She likes watching and making films, and taking photos.

C A R O L   C R E G G

# Derelict

ME AND CLARE were sitting at the edge of the bog, looking at the cutter and the catcher. It was about four in the afternoon and the sky was blue and huge with nothing to hinder it but the boulders on the landscape and the notches of bungalows in the distance. The big curving dome of sky and all the land and us underneath it glowed in sunshine that felt bright and colourful, like a Technicolor movie. We were smoking a packet of cigarettes, one of our first. I'd never seen a cutter and a catcher before, because everywhere else in the country the turf is pressed into long bars by machine. Big yellow tractors couldn't get into the Donegal bogs because the ground was too wet, and too spattered with boulders dropped off when the last glacier tore through Ireland twelve thousand years ago. The two men working the peat were too far away to be able to hear their conversation, but something in the air carried to us the soft sucking sound of the cutter slicing down with the right-angle spade into the wet mud. He heaved the sod over his shoulder to the other man waiting behind him to catch it and set it in a neat row. We were hypnotised by the rhythm of it, the perfect co-ordination between the two of them. With no wind, the smoke from our cigarettes streamed continuously up to heaven.

Danny came along after a while and sat down. We heard him walking up behind us, but we didn't turn or put out our cigarettes in case it was a teacher, because he was the only one who knew we'd be there. When he was about six paces away, I greeted him with the traditional 'Deea Ditch', hello in Irish, which was what we were in Donegal to learn after all. He responded with an equally well timed 'Dig your own fucking ditch.' We only spoke Irish with teachers around, but I always greeted Danny formally, because he loved so much to be able to use the response. Danny was a small wiry guy who didn't get along with the other boys in his house because at fourteen he was a couple of years younger than most of them, and they slagged him off because he hadn't put on his growth spurt yet. But me and Clare were delighted they didn't like him because that meant that he could hang around with us.

'Give us a smoke,' he said. Clare opened her packet and handed him one, and then passed over the box of matches.

'Thanks, bitch.' Danny fancied Clare.

'No problem, fuckface.' Clare liked Danny too. I laughed.

'Are you going to the Ceilidh tonight?' he asked.

'Yeah, course. They'll probably take the roll anyway.'

'Why don't we skip it and just hang around ourselves?'

'Because we'll be killed if they catch us mitching off,' Clare said. She wasn't a natural rule-breaker.

'They already took the roll for classes this morning. They'll not take it twice in one day. Come on, it'll be fun.'

I looked over at Clare, knowing that she was torn between not wanting to get in trouble, and wanting to spend time with Danny.

'I'll go if Clare's going,' I said to help her along. I didn't want to spend the night prancing around the hall looking like a prat.

We met up at half past seven at the place where our shortcut through the bog met the road. From the top of the hill we saw Danny waiting, and we ran the last hundred yards to meet him. The ground flew away quicker and quicker as I ran, until my legs couldn't keep up and I fell and tumbled down the last bit. Clare stopped short to see if I was hurt, but the ground was soft and caught me safely, so she laughed, and I laughed too because I had fallen and wasn't hurt. Danny climbed the fence to give me a hand up.

'Where are we going?' I asked.

'It's a secret.'

So we started walking, heading back up the hill and left instead of right. Midges had come out with the cool of evening. We slapped them dead on our arms when they landed. Me and Clare tagged behind a little as Danny led us through ditches and over barbed wire fencing, until we got to a field with the shell of a house in the middle. There were cows in the field, and the ground was pocked with their hoofprints and their drying pats. It took us a while to get to the house because the ground broke up under our shoes and made us slow down. It had its own presence in the field in the half light of the long evening, and I was terrified because I knew that all the ghosts that had been banished by electricity from the cities had ended up here, in the loneliest places in the world. We walked around to the door. It was off its hinges and rested sideways over the threshold, its sky-blue paint scattered around it in peeled-off shards. We stepped over and went inside. It took a few seconds of blinking to get used to the darkness. Light wandered in from slipped slates on the roof and helped us adjust to indoors. It had been dry weather for weeks, but the house smelled wet and damp. I sat down on a chair in the corner and lit a cigarette. Parts of the ceiling were littered over the cement floor. From my seat I could make out the emptiness of the only other room, papered with the same monotonous Fifties wallpaper. Clare walked over and straightened the photographs on the wall before sitting down beside the hearth. The darkness was pressing in on me. I tried to keep my eyes away from the picture of the Sacred Heart of Jesus looking at me compassionately from over the fireplace. The hearth and plastic-coated kitchen table were too homely, too real. Their loneliness was unbearable. The dresser's bottom drawer had been pulled out onto the floor. In it I could see a copybook open at the irregular verbs in Irish. *Speak, be, take, hear.* They were written carefully in a steady hand in alphabetical order, all in Gaelic script. The dark silence made me think of the sunken Titanic. In twenty years, the only thing that had travelled enough to put this place out of order was the wind. If the world has edges, one of them is here. To stop myself staring at the picture of three children on the wall, I flicked my gaze from Danny to Clare.

'There are ghosts here,' I said.

'I'll light a fire,' Danny said.

'That'll bring them.'

He broke up a chair and put it in the grate. After searching around in the other drawers of the dresser, he found some old issues of *Ireland's Own* and shoved them in amongst the broken furniture. He lit the papers and the room brightened, chasing shadows back behind the dresser and my armchair. He shuffled over and sat down next to Clare.

'This place is scary,' I said. I wanted to get back to the hall, and the stupid music, and the prattish dancing.

'I think it's kind of cosy,' Clare said.

'Why would you just leave a house?' I asked. I couldn't believe they weren't being affected by the desolation of the place, the abandonment.

'Dunno,' Danny said. 'Emigration.'

'But you don't just leave a house, do you?'

'I think you do. No-one wants it except us. Relax, I have a trick. Did you bring your vodka?'

'Course.' I took out the vodka and handed it over to him.

'Watch.' He took out a packet of Lucozade energy sweets. He handed one over to me and gave one to Clare. It was white and powdery. I stuck it in my mouth, it tasted like citrus icing sugar.

'It's just sugar.'

'Nope,' Danny said. 'It's glucose, the most digestible type of sugar there is. Watch.' He tore down the paper of the packet and put ten energy sweets into his mouth at the same time, chewing them up quickly, spitting out flecks of caked sugar. I watched while he slowly unscrewed the vodka as he chewed up the sweets.

'Sláinte.' He winked and began to pour the vodka down his throat. He took two long draughts before he broke into a compulsive fit of coughing, holding the bottle by the neck at arm's length. As soon as he recovered, he emptied the rest of the energy sweets into his mouth, and began to chew as furiously as before.

'What happens now?' asked Clare.

'Five minutes. Makes you high. Try it.'

He handed her a full packet of sweets, and threw another to me. I was annoyed that Danny was wasting his money on sweets instead of cigarettes, but at the same time I wanted to try the glucose-vodka trick. I'd been drunk, and cigarettes made me lightheaded, but that was everyday stuff. It sounded exciting the way Danny had said it. Makes you high. Try it.

I stared over at him. His head was swaying. His eyes rolled up to his eyebrows. I could feel the room closing in on me. Shadows from the fire danced maniacally about us in a wind that whistled in from the roof. I began to get a pain in my stomach as I felt the adrenaline rushing through my blood.

'Jesus fuck.' I slid my nail down one side of the sweets and stuffed half the packet in my mouth. The powdered sugar sucked the wetness from my tongue. I chewed the mess up into swallowable pieces, then took the vodka from Danny's now careless hand. Standing in front of the fire, I stared right into Jesus' eyes and raised the bottom of the vodka bottle up to point at him. I drank till I thought I was going to choke. Clare, already munching energy sweets in preparation, took the bottle off me. I opened the rest of the sweets and dropped them in. The sugar soaked up vodka until I was left sucking a large paste of vodka-flavoured citrus sugar. I collapsed back into my chair to wait for the concoction to absorb into my system. Danny had stood up and was pacing the room, looking at the pictures. I began to feel very awake, and very drunk. Danny stood up on the table and grabbed one of the rafters.

'Don't,' Clare said. He grinned and grabbed the beam with his other hand, then swung one of his legs over too.

'Careful.'

'Get down out of that, you fucking spare,' I said to his left boot, which was dangling in front of my face. He dropped his right hand to give me the fingers, but lost the grip with his left. The top of his body tumbled backwards in a swing which he quickly stopped by grabbing the table. He pulled himself back up on the beam, properly this time, until he was standing on it. He had to stoop over to stop himself from hitting the rafters.

'You'll break your neck.'

He stood up at the biggest gap in the slates so that the top of his body was outside.

We heard his muffled voice shouting into the evening. 'Cool.'

'Come down, Danny.' Clare's face stared upwards, worried. He disappeared out onto the roof. The slates groaned as rusty pins holding them to their rafters bent to take his weight.

'Fucking tosser,' I said. I got up to go outside and look at him on the roof, but before I could reach the door, we heard the clatter of slipped tiles, followed quickly by slipped Danny. We ran outside to where he was lying crumpled up on the grass.

'Daniel,' I shouted.

I glanced quickly at Clare. Her face had on it an expression I'd never seen before. Through the surging of sugar and alcohol I could feel it on my face too. We ran over to Danny. He opened his eyes and blinked up at us.

'What the fuck are you looking at?' he said.

'Fuck you anyway, Daniel. Jesus.'

He rolled neatly forward and stood up.

'I'm going back to the hall,' I said. It was getting darker and I didn't want to go back into the house.

'Christ, you're not thick with me now, are you?'

'No. Though I should be.'

'Come inside till we finish the vodka.'

'Fine.'

I went back inside and sat down. Again the walls began to creep in on me. I opened the vodka and took three great gulps before passing it on, convinced that its effect on my brain would send the walls back and the desolation away.

'I can't believe I didn't break anything,' Danny said.

'Well you must have broke your brain long before, anyway,' I said.

'That was cool. You must have fell seven foot, and just bounced.' Clare's head was reeling too. She was swaying from side to side.

'It must be the ground.'

'Maybe you're just lucky.'

I was trying to concentrate on the conversation, but in the firelight the photos were working their own magic. I forgot what was being said as I became convinced the figures in the pictures were moving when I looked at them out of the corner of my eye. Danny began to pace, picking up bits of wood and broken furniture on the floor, throwing them into the fire. He walked over to the wall and took the picture of the three children off the wall. I watched him look at it for a few seconds and walk over to the fire with it. Overcome with a horror of what he was about to do, I used the one word I swore I'd never use, the one swearword I hated to hear. I heard my voice speaking and it didn't sound like mine.

'Throw that in the fire, you cunt, and I'll slit your fucking throat.'

Danny was taken aback. 'What's got into you?'

'Don't you realise what this place is? It's a graveyard. It's a fucking graveyard.' Danny looked at me, walked slowly back over to the wall and put the picture back on the nail. 'I'm going back,' I said. 'Sorry.' I looked at Clare to see if she was coming.

'See you later,' she said.

'See you tomorrow,' Danny said.

I walked out the door as Danny went over and sat down beside Clare, putting his arm around her shoulders.

'Bye.'

I started running as soon as I knew Clare and Danny couldn't see me. About halfway through the first field my jiggered breathing forced me to stop for a minute and look back. There were glimpses of inky blue through the missing slates and a yellow glow from the windows. I squeezed my knuckles into the stitch in my side and started running again. It was a long jog back to the hall with dusk bleeding into night. The vodka had robbed me of every trace of co-ordination. I tripped on the boggy grass. I fell in the ditch trying to get over the barbed wire fence.

Once I got to the shortcut trail, I calmed down a little and slowed my pace to give me time to sober up. Day was cooling down. I began to feel underdressed in my t-shirt. My arms itched hellishly where midges had bitten. Across the road from the hall, I watched in shadows until the teachers had stopped patrolling outside. Then I walked slowly over to the back door, where I felt safe. If anyone asked what I was doing, I could always say I had just come out for some air. My watch said ten o'clock. It was time for the last few dances. Over the Tannoy, the high treble sound of *The Siege of Ennis* scratched away over ancient speakers. I could hear two teachers inside the door, talking quickly in the fast northern dialect that hid whatever quiet scandal they were discussing.

A soft light streamed out of the window above my head. Even the midges were desperate to be inside. They threw themselves against the electric glow on the glass. I pushed the door open a crack and slid into the hall. Smells of pine and dust hung in the air, unfastened from the floorboards by the stamping of a hundred pairs of shoes. The room was heavy with sweat and laughter. They were having the time of their lives.

**Daniel Pearson** is a native and resident of Mystic, Connecticut, and graduated in 1994 from Bowdoin College. He is currently working on a novel called *White Doom*.

DANIEL PEARSON

# Frosty's Donuts

UPON HEARING that there were fresh and flaky cake donuts, Malky and Wakefield walked downtown to the source. But Frosty's Donut shop on Main Street was closed. Odd for a Monday morning, they thought, a time traditionally associated with donuts. But not unheard of. Fair enough. And so, they returned the next day. Closed again. Curious. They read the hours: Monday through Saturday, 6 a.m.- 3 p.m.; Sundays 5 a.m.-Noon. Odd, they thought, there were no signs about holiday closings or victims of the flu bug. No paper plate taped to the door scribbled with an explanation. Only darkness and a takeout menu. The menu was unremarkable. In addition to donuts, Frosty's sold bran muffins, cheese Danish, bologna sandwiches, glazed crullers, Russian rye, pumpernickel bread, coffee, hot chocolate, RC Cola, tea, homemade soup, and footlong heroes (made on request). Their interest piqued, however, Malky and Wakefield returned again. And again. They walked by at dawn, at dusk, in the middle of the afternoon during the lunch rush, Wednesday at four, Sunday at nine, even stumbling out of the pub late one Friday evening. Their desire for the donuts intensified. But each time they arrived at Frosty's, they found the shop closed. No explanation.

This shouldn't have been a problem. After all, businesses, especially restaurants and cafés, opened and closed without warning. But some time, and in some way, Frosty's definitely opened for business. Malky had seen people on the Town Green drinking coffee out of styrofoam Frosty's Donuts cups. Frosty's sponsored a Little League baseball and softball team, and catered all of the Mahoosuc Valley Board of Education and City Council meetings. Clint, the elderly man in the frayed poplin suit who hung around outside the cigar store, told Wakefield that he ate a Frosty's donut for breakfast every single day of the year. "Even when I was in the hospital with the bypass and that quack

17

told me to lay off the Frosty's, my buddy Gary still snuck me a dozen." Similar testimonials were delivered by bartenders, pharmacists, and teachers, all praising the airy goodness and buttery reliability of the Frosty's donut. But try as they might, Malky and Wakefield couldn't get a taste. They considered calling the shop, but the number was unlisted. The operator at Directory Assistance couldn't find a Frosty's Donuts in Mahoosuc, Maine, or, for that matter, anywhere in Maine. They asked Clint to describe the taste, but he said it was "too damn good for words."

By late October, Malky and Wakefield were despondent. Then, a curious and inexplicable event strengthened their resolve.

It had become customary for Wakefield and Malky to swing by Frosty's no matter what their errand or time schedule. Sometimes they passed by three, four, even five times a day. They had become hardened to the fact that Frosty's would not be open, but they refused to concede. And so, one day in early November, driving back from the lumberyard, Wakefield turned his car onto Main Street expecting, as usual, to see the donut shop in darkness. But when the car passed by Frosty's, Wakefield slammed on the brakes and skidded to a stop, leaving a smoking patch of tire rubber burning on Main Street.

The sight across the road was unbelievable. Frosty's wasn't dark, but packed with customers. Every stool at the counter and every one of the vinyl window booths were filled with patrons reading newspapers, slurping soup, drinking coffee, and, most important of all, biting into beautiful brown Frosty's Donuts. For a few moments, Wakefield was too dumbfounded to move the car, but he soon regained composure and sped up Main Street to find a parking place. There were no spaces on the street, so he raced a few more blocks and two streets over to park in the lot behind the bank. Wakefield didn't even take the time to turn off the engine. He and Malky jumped out of the car, hurdled the shrubbery, dodged around parked cars and post boxes, and sprinted down Main Street toward Frosty's.

When they were within a few blocks, Wakefield shouted to Malky, "I can smell it, I can smell it already." Indeed, there was an alluring, almost sensual warmth, in the Main Street air. But when they arrived at Frosty's, the shop was closed. Completely shut. No trace of life inside, no vestige of fresh baked goods, not even a lingering scent of pumpernickel or Russian rye toasting in the oven. The neon Frosty's sign no longer glowed in the window. And the customers, who only moments before had been reading morning papers and dunking donuts, had disappeared. Wakefield looked at his watch. Frosty's had closed in 220 seconds.

"Did you see? Did they have jelly donuts, or just plain?" Malky asked, panting after the run. "Even that much, even that morsel of information could be useful."

"I couldn't say, it all happened so fast," Wakefield said. "I don't know what I saw."

"What about coating?" Malky asked. "Were the donuts frosted?"

"Another valid question," Wakefield said. "Another valid question I can't answer."

The incident in early November not only focused their desire for a Frosty's donut, it also amplified and confounded their expectations of what the donut would actually taste like. A Frosty's donut was no longer just a heartstopping breakfast pastry with a hole in the middle. It was an ambrosial and transcendental culinary life force, a grail, a doughy icon worthy of worship and understanding. Sitting in their dorm room, Malky and Wakefield often compared the joys of sex, intoxication, fame, immortality, and invisibility, with the exultation they imagined they might experience when biting into a Frosty's donut. Malky said he would rather have a Frosty's donut than the all-time high score on the House of the Dead pinball game. Wakefield said he would trade his most prized possessions, his autographed copy of John Coltrane's 'New Thing at Newport' and his 1978 replica San Diego Padres uniform, for two dozen donuts. If forced to choose, Malky said he would rather be able to fly than have a Frosty's donut. But, he told Wakefield, he would rather have a Frosty's donut than the vertical ability to dunk a basketball.

The Frosty's donut soon became to Malky and Wakefield a form of currency and an exacting assessment of value. If, for example, a meal in the dining hall was particularly good, Wakefield would rate it as worth twenty donuts. A memorably beautiful sunset might qualify as thirty donuts, while the landscape and scenery after the first snowfall, which fell in mid November, was calculated as "at least seventy donuts." Donut-based questions regarding time travel and the afterlife were also proposed: "How many donuts would you give," Malky might ask, for example, "to go back in time to see Josh Gibson or Jackie Robinson playing baseball at the top of their game?" One morning, when he woke up with an oppressive hangover after drinking several pitchers of mojitos the night before, Wakefield said that his throbbing head and churning stomach felt like "a negative baker's dozen."

After the November incident, their conversations were also dominated by theories and postulates about Frosty's elusive hours and modes of operation. Malky reasoned that Frosty's was not in fact open to the public but, rather, that it served as an off-site canteen, cafeteria, or break area for one of the manufacturing firms located along the river. Perhaps it was a second or third shift lounge. Wakefield, who was especially jarred by the November incident, comforted himself in the belief that the donut shop was actually the Community Center designated meeting place for alcoholics, sexaholics, hypnophobes, bulimics, agoraphobes, and other self-help groups. One night, drinking black-and-tans in a hotel bar, Malky drew a crude blueprint and a series of structural schematics on a cocktail napkin to explain how Frosty's was, in fact, a traffic school for those who had been arrested for drinking and driving. Behind the bakery part of the shop, Malky believed, was a screening room where DWI offenders viewed gory car crash videos. After the screenings, he concluded, the offenders then adjourned to the restaurant part of the shop to talk through their problems over coffee and donuts. Malky also thought the shop could be a front for The Fire Baptized Shilohites, a religious cult which funded missionary efforts by performing puppet shows.

After a class trip to the Massachusetts Museum of Contemporary Arts in North Adams, a collection of galleries featuring avant garde, minimalist, and abstract works, Wakefield proposed the idea that Frosty's Donuts was not actually a donut shop but a complicated and subtle work of performance art intended to expose the false idols of globalization and American consumerism. Frosty's was, in Wakefield's words, a "brilliant and innovative commentary on human aspiration."

"Think about it. It makes sense," Wakefield said. "Think of all the freaks and all the artists that live out on the islands off Pemetegoit and Phippsburg."

Malky, however, quickly rejected this theory. "Do you think that these artists would be smart or detailed enough to involve Clint and all the other old people?"

"No, no." Wakefield conceded that his theory, like all their theories, lacked substance and evidence. There was no viable explanation for Frosty's enigmatic and enduring closure.

Dissatisfied with their own philosophizing, Malky and Wakefield began interrogating people on the street. Any time they saw someone eating a donut, any donut, or sipping from a styrofoam Frosty's Donuts cup, they would confront the individual with questions, including: "At what exact time and on what exact day did you buy that donut?" "Would you describe the donut as dry or perhaps as the best donut you have ever tasted?" "Would it be possible for either myself, or my friend, to taste a bit of your donut?" Or, "How did you know, or how do you ever know, when you will be able to buy donuts at Frosty's?"

Responses to these questions were uniform in their deliberate lack of assistance. When asked about Frosty's, people in Mahoosuc would immediately go dumb, or, to avoid having to break off a piece of their donut, they would stuff the remaining portion in their mouth. Elderly people, sitting at midday in the gazebo, often feigned deafness or slumber. Others would mumble unintelligible words through a mouthful of chewed Frosty's donut. Some, bolder and more theatrically furtive, would simply respond to each question with, "Oh, you know, you know." Even a policeman, eating a donut on foot patrol, evaded the issue. When Malky and Wakefield approached the patrolman, he quickly switched on his walkie talkie to assure his dispatcher that he was nearly done "securing the perimeter."

"Did you ever notice?" Malky asked Wakefield one day. "Old people in the park never feed the crumbs of their donuts to the squirrels and pigeons."

"Interesting," Wakefield said. "And did you ever notice that when they're done eating their Frosty's donuts, they fold up the bag and put it back in their pockets?"

Undeterred, they continued to probe and investigate. If they saw a person lurking anywhere near Frosty's entrance on Main Street, one or the other would casually and confidently walk up and say, as if he was a welcome and knowing member of the Frosty's community, "Wonderful day for a donut, isn't it?" These greetings were usually met with raised shoulders and nervous shakes of the head. Everyone in Mahoosuc seemed to be in league against Malky and Wakefield. But what could they hope to hide?

One afternoon, making their usual rounds, Malky and Wakefield saw a man in checkered pants and a chef's jacket smoking outside Frosty's. This was significant. If in fact he was in Frosty's employ, he would represent the first non-customer sighting and the first chance to corner someone on the inside. Perhaps this was the breakthrough Malky and Wakefield had been counting on for weeks. It was a delicate situation. How could they approach the chef without scaring him away? Surely, he had been alerted to their line of questions. They huddled and plotted.

A tactic was determined.

While Wakefield hid behind a car, Malky walked up to the chef and asked for a cigarette, which he was given without delay. After a few puffs, Malky said, as hastily rehearsed just moments before, "The only thing better than a cigarette, is a cigarette and a donut. But I probably don't have to tell you, do I?" Malky waited for a response. The man in the chef's jacket laughed uncomfortably, looked up and down the street a few times, and then, beginning in a jog, but soon breaking into a full gallop, sprinted toward the river.

Malky hailed Wakefield, who emerged from behind the parked car. "Split up, split up," Wakefield yelled. "Take the Cribstone bridge and I'll try to cut him off at the plating works." From the top of Main Street, they could see the chef heading for the lumberyard, brick factories, and the hydroelectric plant. Wakefield ran down Federal Street anticipating that the chef might try to cross the river over the freight rail bridge. Seeing that the chef had turned right, Malky also raced for the train line. The chef, nimble and adept, hopped over tracks and railroad ties, until he realized that Malky and Wakefield were closing in from both sides. Jumping down several feet, onto a rocky path lined with nettles and scrap metal, the chef searched for an opening among corrugated metal warehouses and the hydroelectric plant. Malky and Wakefield leaped off the tracks. Escape seemed impossible. Within only seconds, the chef disappeared, lost among wire spools and sonic turbines.

The flight of the chef, the most revealing and incriminating evidence that Frosty's was more than just a neighborhood donut shop, inspired Malky and Wakefield to take their questions to Tesso, the owner of Tesso's Variety.

It was generally agreed by both locals and students that Tesso, more than anybody else, knew everything. Tesso, a diminutive Italian, whose family came from Calabria, was chairman of the Planning and Zoning Commission, co-chair of the Democratic Town Committee, chair of the Mahoosuc School Renovation and Expansion Committee, past president of the Mahoosuc Rotary, and the executive director of the Pasammaquoddy Bay Historical Society. Once a semester, Tesso was also invited by the college's Italian department to lecture on the politics of the Vatican. Every morning, Tesso woke up at dawn, walked six miles, and then finished his exercise with a dip in the icy waters of the Mahoosuc River. Every day after dinner, Tesso claimed that he ate a raw egg mixed in a glass of brandy. But he attributed the vitality of his constitution and the gravity-defying ascension of his jet black pompadour to a diet rich in olive oil and buttermilk.

Malky and Wakefield had often used Wakefield's fake New Mexico state I.D. to purchase beer and wine at Tesso's. The Variety shopkeeper knew that they were underage. It didn't matter. Age, except in wine and cheese, was of no consequence to him.

It was Tesso who told Malky and Wakefield about the sledding hills in Topsham, the library of rare manuscripts in the Susan Dwight Bliss Room, the trout streams and ice-fishing huts in Gardiner, the arrowheads and carved stones on Damariscotta Neck, and the outdoor ice-hockey rink in the Sewer District. Tesso had alerted them to the cash machine in Mahoosuc Bay that dispensed one and five dollar bills. It was Tesso who instructed the two friends how to make out the faces and heads on the rock formations in the quarry.

Tesso held nothing back. He loved all of Mahoosuc. Even though he had a stake in the local food economy, it was Tesso who told Malky and Wakefield about the all-you-can-eat Truckers Breakfast at The Mahoosuc Diner, the Bloody Mary's made with Dijon and wasabi in the bar at the Maine Line Hotel, the littlenecks at Palmer Landing Marina, and the fish chowder at the Dolphin. And, most importantly, it was Tesso who first suggested that Malky and Wakefield walk down Main Street to enjoy a Frosty's donut. Tesso had nothing to hide.

Now that his daughters were old enough to be trusted with the deli and the cash register, Tesso spent most of his time sipping and sampling Italian wines in the Variety basement. After the incident with the chef, Malky and Wakefield went without delay to Tesso's market on Pleasant Street. When they entered the shop, Gabriella, Tesso's older daughter, looked up from a slab of parma, pointed with a cleaver, and said, "He's downstairs."

Wakefield opened a hatch and the two friends descended by way of a ladder. Through the dim light of a single apple-scented candle, they found Tesso seated on a crate, slicing up a pungent block of goat's cheese. An orange, a tomato, and loaf of bread lay sectioned before him. The basement was full of unopened crates of wine, liqueurs, olive oils, pistachios, and imported beers. Cured meats, suspended in mesh and netting, hung from the ceiling.

Tesso lit another candle and offered Malky and Wakefield the choice of a robust Chianti or a muscatel. They selected the red and pulled up a crate.

"Tesso," Wakefield said. "You know we have never doubted you."

"Yes, I know this," said Tesso, lifting a cork to his nose.

"You suggested that we should go to Frosty's, and we have been to Frosty's, many times, but it is never open," Wakefield said. "But we know it is open, because we have seen that it is open, and smelled the baking bread, and seen the donuts consumed in the park."

"And the bread, what do you remember of the bread?" Tesso said.

"I remember the smell. It tantalized me. When I smelled it, I ran to it."

"Yes, but you dream of the donuts?" Tesso said. "You imagine they will be good."

"Yes. They must be good."

Tesso nodded in tacit assent.

"You are anxious for the donuts," Tesso said. "But when you go to Frosty's, it is empty and often dark."

"Yes, but more than just darkness," Wakefield said. "When we ask people to tell us when we may go to Frosty's, they look away. Sometimes, they even run away."

Tesso leaned forward.

"Then you have seen the chef?"

"Not more than ten minutes ago," Malky said. "Smoking."

Tesso laughed and drank a healthy draught from his glass. Malky drank as well, swirling the wine around in his mouth. He tasted the lightness of grapefruit, cedar, smoke, perhaps cherry. But the ultimate sensation was flat and featureless. The wine, even to his uneducated palate lacked body and soul. This was not one of the Variety's better vintages.

"It is not to worry," Tesso said. "There will be donuts. There will always be donuts."

"Yes, but when?" Wakefield asked.

Tesso put down his glass, rubbed the bridge of his nose, and seemed to withdraw from the moment. Then, after a few seconds in meditation, he opened his eyes.

"You see all around me the products of Italy." Tesso gestured to the crates and meats. "You must ask yourself why a Florentine oil lacks the spirit of the Calabrese."

"I don't know. But there must be factors of climate and soil," Wakefield said.

"Perhaps, but what of Parma ham?" Tesso asked. "Only a ham from Parma may travel under that appellation. It is the same as champagne from Rheims and Cuban cigars."

"I understand," Malky said.

"A grape is not a fig," Tesso said. "A mango is not a kiwi."

"Yes, but what of the donuts?" Wakefield said. "What is the secret?"

"There is no secret," Tesso said. "You will know this when you taste the donuts."

"Yes, but when? When can we taste the donuts?" Malky said.

"Maybe today. Maybe tomorrow. Perhaps next week," Tesso said. "I cannot tell you when there will be donuts. I know only that there will be donuts, and you will have them."

Wakefield finished his glass in one gulp, leaning his head way back, and noticed a neatly folded white wax-paper Frosty's Donuts bag lying on the floor behind Tesso. He grabbed it and opened it. Only a dusting of crumbs fell out. He handed it to Malky, who observed that the bag was unmarked by grease stains. This told volumes. Tesso laughed.

"Tesso, please, do you have any donuts left?" Wakefield asked.

Again Tesso laughed. He turned his body away from the two friends, turned back around, and then extended his left hand, which was empty.

"What is that?" Malky asked.

"This is all I can offer you," he said, restraining a smile. "Donut holes."

The Tesso's incident convinced Malky and Wakefield that they were alone in their pursuit of the Frosty's donut. Undaunted, they resolved to hold all-night vigils until they witnessed, with their own eyes, somebody opening Frosty's. One Friday evening, after dinner, therefore, the two drove down Main Street and parked Wakefield's station wagon across the street from Frosty's. The car was packed with sleeping bags, bottled water, a case of Old German beer, apples, bread, and binoculars. Wakefield brought a hand-held tape recorder and notebook to keep a log of activity in and around the donut shop. They intended to camp out in the car, each taking six hour shifts on guard duty. They did not expect to stay in the car for more than twenty-four hours. If necessary, however, they were prepared to remain until the following Tuesday evening, when the Bruins played the Nordiques on television. Malky and Wakefield never missed a Bruins hockey game.

The first night in the car, both Malky and Wakefield kept watch. A few drunks stumbled past the donut shop and a few teenage kids hid down the alley between Frosty's and the Sir Tux formal wear rental shop to take nitrous hits from whipped cream cans. But other than that, there was little to report. During the second day, Malky and Wakefield drifted in and out of sleep or listened to the radio. Every few hours, one of the two would take a walk around the block to stretch their legs. Again, during the second night, there was little activity to report. Suprisingly, Sunday, the third straight day sleeping in the car, also passed without event. By Sunday night, Malky and Wakefield began to think that their presence was preventing the production of Frosty's donuts. "At this point," Wakefield said into the hand-held tape recorder, "I have to wonder if production has not been moved to a safe house, perhaps a Frosty's annex or some undisclosed location away from our prying eyes." Malky began to think that Frosty's went to extreme lengths of secrecy to preserve a magical recipe for donuts. This was possible, Wakefield said. But where was Tesso? Surely, in three days, they would have seen the bakery in some form of operation. Surely, they would have seen Clint making his way down to Frosty's for his daily fix. The third night in the car was passed in anxiety. Were Malky and Wakefield being watched? And, where was the chef?

During the course of the third night, Malky found himself cataloguing all the donuts and pastries he had ever tasted. Love Knots. Cheese Danish. Boston Cremes. Crullers. Jelly. Jelly glazed. Glazed. Chocolate filled. Chocolate. Apple Turnovers. Coconut Cream. Napoleons. Eclairs. It was easy to describe each one in terms of content, shape, and texture, but what made one donut or pastry better than another? Malky had eaten donuts in diners, bakeries, supermarkets and cafés up and down the east coast, but they blurred together in his memory as one caked mass of brown dough. But the Frosty's donut, the elusive donut they had sought for months, seemed different. He tried to shake his mind free of the Frosty's donut, tried to lump it in with all the others, but he could not contain his imagination. There was only sleep, which Malky soon succumbed to, even though it was his shift on guard duty.

At some point during the night, the sound of a car engine dying, and then the rattling of keys, roused Malky from his slumber. He looked across the street. Someone was shutting the driver's door of a Buick Century sedan and walking toward the Frosty's entrance. In silhouette, the individual appeared to be wearing the pointed, steeple-crowned hat of a Puritan magistrate. But when the individual turned to the streetlight to shut the car door, Malky realized the figure was that of a woman with a towering beehive hairdo.

Malky looked at his watch. It was 4:30 a.m. He punched Wakefield on the arm and, when his friend opened his eyes, pointed across the street. The beehive woman was then inserting a key into the front door of Frosty's Donuts. There was no hesitation.

"Go", Wakefield said. "Go."

They sprinted across the street, just as the beehive woman switched on the neon Frosty's sign. Then, she flipped the CLOSED sign around to read OPEN. Malky and Wakefield each took a seat on one of the spinning stools around the counter. The lights in the shop went on. It had finally happened. They were inside Frosty's Donuts.

Frosty's interior resembled most donut shops. Checkered table-cloths. Spinning padded vinyl counter stools and vinyl booths. Laminated menus paperclipped with specials. Every napkin dispenser, every counter top, every refrigeration surface, and every piece of stainless steel cookery, cutlery, and coffee brewing equipment was spotless. The restaurant felt cool and airy, like the main branch of a savings bank. The walls of the shop were decorated with nineteenth-century logging competition photos, sepia-tinted browns and whites of giant men in buttered boots rolling white pines down Main Street. Dozens of photos of Frosty's Donuts Little League baseball teams hung behind the counter. Little League baseball trophies and a vintage Moxie clock stood on a shelf near a stack of coffee mugs inscribed with 'Frosty's In Mahoosuc — A Friend For Life.' People in Maine swore by Moxie soda, as both a tonic and a hangover cure. Malky had tried to make himself enjoy it, but there was no getting around it. Moxie tasted like the smell of ear medicine.

The beehive woman, who was wearing a white blouse, white skirt, white apron, and white orthopedic shoes, appeared before them like a Pentecostal missionary. She stood motionless, as polished and porcelain as the shop's interior. Malky took a good long look at her as she leaned against an empty rack of donuts. Once he looked at her face, she seemed far less ceramic. She could have been fifty or maybe sixty, but there was nothing funny about the laugh lines streaking out from her eyes and mouth. A youthful liquidity in her motion suggested that the lines were a by-product of hard living. It wasn't the clock ticking away, but the odometer. She had mileage. Malky looked at her name-tag. It said: Ludella B.

Without being asked, Ludella placed two steaming cups of coffee in front of Malky and Wakefield. They poured cream into their coffee and conferred. It was decided to order one of everything on the menu, including a dozen donuts for the shop and a dozen to go.

"What kind of bread do you have today?" Wakefield asked Ludella.

"Bread?" she said. "What are you talking about?"

"It says on the menu that you have a special daily bread. What kind of bread?"

The waitress looked nervously back toward the bakery and kitchen.

"Listen, don't start with the bread bit, okay," she said, shaking her finger at the two customers. "You start with the bread bit, especially this time of morning, and I'm going to hear about it from the man in the back. Is that what you want?"

"Okay, I apologize," Wakefield said. "We'll have one dozen donuts."

Ludella went through the swinging door to the bakery and returned with a dozen donuts wrapped in a white cardboard box tied with a piece of twine. Malky and Wakefield opened the box and looked inside. There they were. Frosty's donuts. They each removed one, cradling it as if they had unearthed a dinosaur's egg. Here was the moment they had waited weeks and weeks for. The donuts appeared hefty, sweet, and substantial. All the anticipation, all the hope and frustration, all Frosty's mystery had been stripped down to this moment. Malky and Wakefield tapped their donuts together and then they each took a bite.

The donuts were stale. Rock hard. No, couldn't be, they thought. They bit again. Stale.

"Mine's stale," Malky whispered to Wakefield, while the waitress dusted the trophies.

"Mine's not only stale," Wakefield whispered back. "There's something crunchy and granular in there, like crushed shells or maybe gravel. It tastes like sand."

They tried another donut in the box. Stale again.

"Excuse me," Wakefield said to Ludella. "I don't mean to cause any problems, but these donuts, I think, are a little old. Do you happen to have any fresher donuts?"

To show what he meant, Wakefield tapped the donut on his plate and produced a dull but audible drum roll. The waitress scratched at her beehive with a fork, thought for a minute, and then went through the swinging door to the bakery. Malky and Wakefield heard the mumbles of a verbal exchange between a male and female voice. Then, a man in a billowing white hat and checkered pants soon appeared. It was the chef, sweating and heaving.

"I have received a report, and I feel that you are mistaken," the Chef said.

"Please, we don't mean any disrespect, it's only that these donuts seem a little stale, especially for this time of morning," Wakefield said.

"No, you are again mistaken, the donuts are fresh. I baked them this morning. They have just come from my own hands." The chef held out his floury mitts. He was rocking back and forth like a metronome.

Wakefield tapped the donut on the counter, again producing a staccato beat.

"Listen," Wakefield said. "That is the sound of an old donut."

The chef covered his mouth with his hand in disbelief. He took a deep breath.

"You see, Frosty's donuts are not like other donuts. I'm not at liberty to explain why this is, but it is safe to say that our quality is without compare," the chef said. "Perhaps you have never tasted a donut quite like Frosty's, and so you blame me for your own ignorance."

Again, Wakefield tapped the donut on the counter.

"This donut is stale," Wakefield said. The chef rubbed his hands together.

"Ludella, I am feeling both anger and sadness," the chef said, without looking at her.

"There's reason for anger and sadness," she said. "The donuts ain't stale."

"Listen, I admit that I've never had Frosty's donuts," Wakefield said. "But I have had donuts and many other baked goods. I wouldn't lie about freshness."

"I will admit, I am not familiar with the tastes of the young people. We don't get many people your age in here," the chef said. "But trust me, these donuts are fresh. You will see."

"Now, please understand, I certainly don't mean any disrespect to you or to your donuts," Wakefield said. "But there are simple properties of freshness and staleness that are universally agreed upon, regardless of age. Fresh donuts are soft, supple, like a croissant or a brioche, yet they hold their form in coffee. But this donut, this donut, I could cut diamonds with this donut. Fresh is fresh. But stale is stale. And this donut is stale."

The chef wiped his forehead with an apron.

"Wrong," he said. "I fear you are mistaken."

"No, I am not," Wakefield countered. "The donuts are stale."

"They are fresh, barely an hour old. Just out of the oven, almost too warm to touch."

"Please, just admit that they're stale." Wakefield offered his donut to the chef. "Taste it. Taste it."

The chef stepped away and again wiped his forehead with the bottom of his apron. Then a smile came to his face, as if somewhere in the distance he had heard the first strains of a concerto. He nodded a few times to himself. Ludella nodded as well.

"Yes, you speak of donuts," the chef said, turning to Malky. "But how is the coffee?"

"The coffee is aromatic and rich," Malky said. It was. "Strong, even poignant. I would have a second cup. I would recommend this coffee to a friend."

"It's not the coffee," the chef said. "It's the water."

"It's good coffee either way. But the donuts are still stale."

"So you would return to Frosty's on another occasion?" the chef asked.

"Perhaps," Malky said. "But only if we knew the hours."

"What are you talking about?" the chef said. "The hours are on the door."

"They're on the door, but we've been here many times during business hours and you weren't open," Malky said. "You're never open."

"What? That is impossible," the chef said. "I never miss a day."

"What about the bread?" Wakefield said. "When will there be bread?"

"Bread?" the chef said. He was irate, pounding his fist on the counter. "When will there be bread? Why would you even say such a thing, on a Monday?"

With this the chef returned to the bakery part of the shop. Malky and Wakefield expected that he would return with some token or rejoinder, but he did not. Thirty seconds later, they heard an engine rev and then watched the chef, now wearing goggles and fringed leather riding chaps, speed away on a motorcycle, a cirrus cloud of blue exhaust trailing out of sight. Malky and Wakefield sat in silence for more than two hours, waiting and hoping for other customers to arrive. But no one did. Even when delivery trucks and commuters began to grind their gears up and down Main Street, the shop remained empty. Every one of the donuts in the box was stale. There was something earthy and sedimentary about them, as if they were packed with dirt. It was difficult to stomach the stale donuts, but Malky and Wakefield felt compelled to, almost as a vendetta against the chef. They consumed them by dunking and saturating them in coffee, which they both admitted was truly stellar, memorable coffee.

When the sun rose over the pine trees lining the Mahoosuc River, Malky and Wakefield returned to the car and began the drive back toward the campus. Instead of heading directly up Pleasant Street, however, Wakefield turned the car left into the winding road that followed the river and the rail line out toward the ocean, and then took two more rights so that they were back on Main Street. Malky didn't need to ask where Wakefield was going. In fact, he was relieved that Wakefield shared the curiosity he had been hesitant to articulate.

The station wagon, now littered with empty bottles and sandwich wrappers, moved slowly down Main Street, past the cigar store, the pawn shop that sold broken telephones and expired coupons, and the appliance repair store that always smelled like burning leaves. The parking space where they had slept for three nights remained vacant, so Wakefield parked again across the street from Frosty's. He and Malky looked across the road.

As they somehow expected, Frosty's was heaving with customers. Ludella, a butterfly barrette in her beehive, moved gracefully about the booths, a pad in one hand and a pot of coffee in the other. Senior citizens in sweaters and sky-blue windbreakers occupied the window booths, drinking coffee, solving the jumble, and reading the papers. The chef, no longer goggled or chapped, stood behind the counter holding his belly as he narrated a story to Clint. The chef repeatedly pointed to the two stools formerly occupied by Malky and Wakefield, laughing harder with each gesture to the stools. The laughter carried across the road. FROSTY'S flashed from the illuminated neon sign. A dairy truck was parked to the side of the building, delivering milk, eggs, and butter. The air was redolent of baking bread. The front door opened and Tesso, his hair wet from the river, his body toned and sculpted by his six mile walk, exited onto the street, carrying a white box and a loaf of what appeared to be Italian bread.

A day that began in astonishment and optimism had quickly degenerated into bitterness and confusion. Wakefield did not speak. But Malky felt more than ever that the shop was a front for the puppeteering religious cult. He tried to put his mind inside the deeper and darker workings behind Frosty's friendly family-style facade. Somewhere in that bakery or in a makeshift chapel in the basement beneath the shop, he imagined that the cult conducted mass weddings or unorthodox baptismal services involving Moxie and donut dough. He saw bike after bike of zealot motorcylists riding in tandem down country lanes and forest paths, their beehives and coifs unaffected by the oncoming wind. But if Frosty's was trying to gain new members, why would it persist in peddling a stale and inedible product? And, if Frosty's was in fact the front for a cult, how could Malky explain Tesso's participation? Tesso was one of the leading figures in Mahoosuc's Catholic community, a Knight of Columbus who often passed the plate and organized the St. Mary Star of the Sea youth basketball league and free-throw shooting contest. There was no explanation. Anything was possible.

The initial result of the Frosty's incident was the immediate reversal of the currency and value system based on donuts. By night-time, donuts no longer represented joy and immortality, but pain and disappointment. At one point during the hockey game, for example, when the Nordiques took the lead over the Bruins, Malky remarked that his team was playing "like donuts." When the Bruins' pugnacious defenseman John Haverchuk dropped his gloves and started landing injurious punches to the face of a Nordiques player, Wakefield remarked that Haverchuk was "throwing donuts." By the third period of the game, donuts had evolved into an expletive.

Still, conversations and concerns were dominated by the mystery of the Frosty's donut. When Malky and Wakefield finally retired to bed, after weeks of hypotheses, after three days in the car, after a confusing morning at Frosty's counter, after a last minute loss to the middling Nordiques, the doughy disc lay sphinxlike and foremost in their minds. Lying in the darkness of their dorm room, they did not speak, but each rolled the donut over and over in his thoughts. It could not be dismissed or forgotten as easily as a televised celebrity circus or the inflated price of movie popcorn. Malky and Wakefield could go back to their routine of pinball competitions and street hockey, but how could they walk or drive by Frosty's without wondering what went on in that kitchen. Would they follow the chef on his motorcycle, giving chase on the highway until the bike sputtered out of gas? Would they track Ludella in her Century, hoping she would lead them to a woodland cult service where brainwashed children in checkered pants wore bracelets of donut dough? Who could say?

All of Maine opened up before them. Malky and Wakefield saw the logging roads that led across the Lake of Isles to the historic trapping lands in Ontario and Nova Scotia. They saw the sacred Native American hunting grounds strewn with arrowheads and caribou bones. They saw whitewashed lobster fishing villages, a craggy coastline longer than California, and a granite cathedral at the top of Mount Kathadin. But, as much as they tried to concentrate on the rest of the landscape, as much as they wanted to put the donuts behind them, they could not escape the image of Frosty's neon sign, flashing off and on, off and on.

"What will we do tomorrow?" Malky asked.

"A valid question," Wakefield said. "What will we do tomorrow?"

**Gillian Fyffe** is married with two children. She is a graduate of St Andrews and writes fiction as well as poetry. She lives in Dunino and is now teaching at Fettes College Preparatory School in Edinburgh.

### GILLIAN FYFFE

# Dilemmas of a Courtesan

*A verse-biography of Rose Joseph de la Pagerie or Beauharnais or Bonaparte, the Empress Josephine:*

Germinal: Liberty

*"Come with one of your daughters or with both of them, but hurry."*
        *Aubenas,* Histoire de l'Impératrice

Here is a child who prays that nothing shall
Condemn her to her home in Martinique,
Nor dissolute father nor mother's pique
Induce her to the sons of Porte-Royale.
Her navy eyes might hold a court in thrall
But Paris knows her dowry has been spent
On negro whores, and puberty has meant
Her sisters' youth becomes *le principal.*

If Catherine had not died, and if Manette
Were not the youngest de la Pagerie,
How different would her destiny have been;
Nor would all France recall that languor yet
That marked her as Creole. For Rose *will* be
At first her cousin's bride, and then a queen.

Messidor: Equality

*"Versailles and Paris sent their linen to be washed*
*in Santo Domingo, just as they had their shirts made*
*in Curaçao and their porcelain repaired in China."*
　　　　　　*Masson,* Josephine de Beauharnais

Limestoned and sugared in Saint Honoré!
The tide of Paris' terror still to break,
Beauharnais plans the future he would make,
Renaming and recounting every day.
Soon only ghosts live in the dank Marais
Where once a court of stiff-brocaded rakes
Used all the flour the queen had meant for cakes
For oligarchic powder-puffed display.

New World salons now challenge such excess
By seeding gardens with equality.
Their courtesans reward the new finesse
Of wit and warrior-philosophy.
*Citoyennes* in muslin, their titles quashed,
Send frocks to San Domingo, to be washed.

Thermidor: Fraternity

*"And the crowning of love's tenderest wishes,*
*thanks to darkness and loose clothing."*
　　　　*Sorel,* Le Convent des Carmes

Now *femme du maréchal du camp* has brought
The terror of *Les Carmes.* They come at ten.
Each Tarot dawn she turns *mort ou la reine*
That she might make, because they have forgot
*Americaine* and even *sans-culottes,*
Her vigil for the tumbril driver's cry
In fevered hope that someone else will die
So that the morrow's vigil might be got.

But when some go, and even Beauharnais,
Half-crazed with joy, she damps her gown to give
To wit and lust the hours that she should grieve;
Beds Lazare Hoche, oblivious for a day.
When she is *ci-devant,* she who will live,
She'll search for terrored air, that she may breathe.

Fructidor: Beauharnais

*"The Bal des Victimes were reserved for families*
*of which at least one member had been guillotined."*
                              *Bruce,* Napoleon and Josephine

Knowing him dead, she knows herself alive.
That is her touchstone; only it made real
The livid Thermidor. Condemned to feel
By contrast, far too damaged to derive
Freedom from liberty, she must connive
At frantic pleasure, hazard, fascinate,
Wear ribbon on her throat to celebrate
The guillotine, which taught her to survive.

She had expected love, but once she knew
Herself *femme mal aimée,* she understood
Love's sacrifice was all that would redeem
A future for her son, and daughter too.
All revolutionaries can be wooed
By icons of the *ancien régime.*

Vendémiaire: Lazare Hoche

*"In prison it is perfectly understandable to take a*
*whore as a mistress, but not to make her one's*
*lawful wife."*
　　　　　　*Barras,* Mémoires

Her love for Lazare Hoche survived the coup
Of Thermidor, and simmered in its heat.
Tumbrilled away before the tocsin's beat
Could promise that he'd live the Terror through,
She found him safe but married. Yet she knew
The intellectual-radical elite
Adored her, and would prompt him to compete
For favour as her reputation grew.

She made herself an icon. Destitute
And dangerously old, she ordered gauze
To drape her as a Roman; hired a coach
The laundry-maid must pay, to go barefoot.
This nakedness David had made a *cause*
*Célèbre*. Rose meant it only as reproach.

Brumaire: Paul Barras

*"Mme de Beauharnais, with two children and no*
*money, through hunger and an amorous disposition,*
*had become the* maîtresse en titre *of Barras."*
                                    *Baron de Frenilly*

Lazare had seen her heart and thought it won.
Rose knew the fate of those who love too well:
At thirty-one the fears she'd have to quell,
And though he took as aide her only son,
The risks that her dependency would run.
Only Barras had power to dispel
The rumours that her blackening teeth would tell
Against her. Their liasion was begun.

Men like Lazare, the warrior-elite,
Tall, beautiful, and even sabre-cut,
Make womanhood a matter to rejoice.
Yet men like Paul Barras, cruel and effete,
Negotiate in human passion but
They grant to courtesans a public voice.

Frimaire: Napoleon

*"The marriage would give me consistency, would
make people forget my Corsican name, would
make me wholly French."*

Gourgaud, Mémoires

As Barras' mistress she'd no need to wed.
Such *inconséquence*, Napoleon would say,
Gave him his chance that he might make his way,
Demanding marriage, to an icon's bed.
A man of whom Lazare Hoche had said
*Corsican terroriste!* Barras will pay
All Italy, and Rose de Beauharnais,
To keep Napoleon at the Army's head.

Now Europe's cradled in incestuous hands.
At McDermott's Academy her son,
His brother and a Tallien half-child,
Shared rooms as Bonaparte would share his lands.
She married for the victories he had won.
He married for position, but beguiled.

Nivôse: Hippolyte Charles

*"I left in such a hurry yesterday that
I had no time to leave a message for the
Gardener."*
                Josephine, Lettres to Mme de Kreny

How secret is a lover that his name
Must be disputed over centuries
Till Louis Hastier made out a maze
Of cryptic reference to prove his claim?
And who but Josephine must be to blame?
Yet history will not avert its gaze.
Even an empress cannot quite erase
The madness of the cuckolding of fame.

The carved reliefs have not yet worn away
That show, next to his heir the King of Rome,
Napoleon Bonaparte, and in between
Where Marie Louise ought to be on display,
Legend has given Josephine a home.
No passion's secret for a king or queen.

Pluviôse: Emperor

*"I noticed there was no real enthusiasm anywhere,*
*but then nothing untoward happened either."*
                                    Napoleon, Lettres

His coronation brought her new dismay.
Even his coins, where *République* would hide
With *Empereur* engraved the other side,
Summed up the contradictions of the day.
If he should crown her, others might gainsay
Divorce. In Tuileries he waits the tide
Of tears, but Josephine's imperial pride
Soothes and assures him he will have his way.

What sort of woman is this new empress?
She has become a creature of the state.
Her emperor will soon come to regret
Her infertility. Her critics press.
Together, newly-crowned, they sit till late
In private and adoring tête-à-tête.

Ventôse: Divorce

*"Naturally I would prefer to have my mistress*
*crowned, but I must be allied with sovereigns."*
                                        Remusat, Mémoires

A dynasty must have a royal child.
She knows it. Now that she's been crowned a queen
She would not have her public anguish seen.
And he, although he knows he is reviled,
For all her courtesy and for her mild
Acceptance of the exile this will mean,
Lights up the Tuileries as it has always been,
And by *répudiation* is defiled.

They are not human now. At once she flees
The court that held her bee-embroidered train
For Malmaison, but finding there the man
Who tilts at fate to wed Marie Louise,
They walk the gardens, hand in hand, in rain:
The *terroriste* and his own *courtisane*.

VICTORIA QUINN

# Found Objects

AN INTERVIEW WITH WILL MACLEAN

WILL MACLEAN is one of Scotland's leading contemporary artists. His etchings and three-dimensional artwork are particularly highly-regarded. He is currently a Professor of Fine Arts at Duncan of Jordanstone College of Fine Arts, and his latest multimedia installation, *Driftworks*, is on tour around the United Kingdom

**Q:** Parallels have been drawn between yourself and the Scottish poet, Ian Hamilton Finlay, with his sculptural representations of his concrete poetry. How consciously do you draw on poetry as a source of inspiration?

**A:** I often draw on poetry, especially the poems of Sorley MacLean who is one of the leading Gaelic poets. He writes especially well about the clearances. For me, his key work is *Hallaig*. This has inspired several pieces. Sorley MacLean continued in the tradition of Hugh MacDiarmid. He was writing immediately after the war and was in line for the Nobel Prize for poetry at one point.

**Q:** I read that you never learned Gaelic. Do you feel that your output would have differed in any way, had you been able to? As it stands, it seems to contain so much reaching out after sensed, half-hidden meanings.

**A:** Very much so. It's the major regret of my life. I would have had access to an incredible amount of material, both anecdotal and written. I made a decision a number of years ago. It's such a complex issue – to be a Gaelic learner now, as an academic exercise? I'm not sure. It may be time well spent.

**Q:** Do you prefer drawing on myths and folk-tales, or on writing produced by living authors who may have very fixed ideas about interpretation?

**A:** I prefer the oral tradition. One of the interesting things about Sorley MacLean is that his work has a surreal quality, and some tales from the oral tradition – particularly medieval ones – have that same quality. It's something I'm always looking for when looking at the written word. I mean, if I'm reading a history of travels through the Highlands, I'm into the anecdotes, not the number of villagers.

**Q:** Have you ever created pieces about land-based experiences of the clearances?
**A:** Yes, a small body of work, mainly based on Hallaig: "The windows were barred and shuttered/Where first I saw the west". I've also done a number of pieces called *Window Visitation: North Uist* based on a book of Gaelic mythology by Reverend Grierson. There's a myth that when you die, your soul leaves your body in the form of a butterfly, and that's why I included a butterfly in the construction. Just after I did it I saw a picture of a butterfly and a window by Joseph Cornell. There's a strong visual connection going on there.

**Q:** Which contemporary writers do you find most inspirational?
**A:** Well, Sorely MacLean for a start. He had a great influence on Highland culture. I read mainly histories or biographies. John Marsden's history of Celtic Churches is a wonderful book, although it may be a bit dry in places, but I also like E. Annie Proulx, John Redman and James Hunter. I tend to read books that are going to feed back into the work in some way.

**Q:** In *Cardinal Points*, it is claimed that your previous collections (*Sea Reliquaries, Emigration, Arctic Exploration, Whaling and Fishing*) reflect ongoing themes. Would you say that these themes remain central to your work, or have new subjects come to the fore?
**A:** It's not the themes that have changed, it's the way of relating to them. I am now experimenting with installations and video technology – it's very exciting. I visited Newfoundland and found lots of parallels there with the culture and the fishing industry here in Scotland and that led to my latest exhibition, *Driftworks*.

**Q:** Who do you consider to have been the greatest influence on your work?
**A:** The American artist, Joseph Cornell. He was a surrealist from New York who made boxed constructions which had a strong narrative within them. He was quiet. He stood outside the mainstream. Oh, and Giorgio de Chirico, who is a metaphysical artist. His work is enigmatic and full of implications. My wife, Marian Leven, is an artist too, and she's a big influence on my work. We've been married a long time, and although she's not part of my information-gathering process, she's fundamental to supporting me

emotionally, technically and critically. It's amazing to have someone there who can say, "that's dreadful!"

**Q:** What conditions need to exist for you to be able to create?
**A:** I have a notebook with me most of the time and I jot down ideas, phrases, sentences and sketches. I use it as a kind of 'holding tank.' Unless I want to record a piece of information in, say, a museum, I tend not to draw for the sake of drawing. Almost all of my work is done in my studio, apart from the etching. I do that here, at Dundee Contemporary Arts.

**Q:** As I understand it, you accidentally stumbled on your ability to carve and construct 3-dimensional objects, but trained in drawing, painting and printmaking. What do you find most satisfying?
**A:** Very much the former. One of the reasons I moved away from oil-painting was because I was never emotionally or temperamentally suited to oils. I need to work quickly and make a lot of changes as I go. I hate watching paint dry. Besides, although I admire the ways other people use colour, it's not the most important thing for me. Technology now allows a lot more freedom. If I had gone through art school now, I would be a totally different artist as there's much more mixed media work being done. There was very little of that kind of experimentation encouraged in Scotland until the 1970s or 1980s.

**Q:** How do you know which materials to use, when so much of what you are doing has not been done before?
**A:** Most of the stuff I use, I either gathered or it was sent to me. It's found objects, chosen for the sake of the shape or the material. It sits in the sheds at the back of my studio and the sheds are just packed. I tend to work on a dozen things at a time, so I have a rummage until the idea meets something. It can be a simple matter of a compositional device, a shape. I use my sheds as a kind of visual library.

**Q:** What is your favourite medium, and why?
**A:** Co-polymer emulsion. It's a plasticised paint and you can add art or earth pigments to it. Basically, anything that will stick onto the other materials I use!

**Q:** Your later work seems much more densely packed with detail, whereas the earlier pieces seem to capture something of the space found at sea. Do you agree, and if so, is there a conscious cause?
**A:** Yes. The level of detail has become offset by bigger areas of texture, worked areas of paint. It's not so narrative or figurative as it used to be. Sometimes I look back and think,

'I couldn't do that now'. I'm not into that level of craft any longer. My work is more aesthetic, less agenda-driven. I now feel that some of the earlier pieces push the agenda too hard.

**Q:** It is said that writing is a solitary art, regardless of its social content. Do you consider the same to be true of the visual arts?
**A:** Yes. I'm faced with a blank piece of paper in the same way you are.

**Q:** What have been your experiences of collaboration, its benefits and its pitfalls?
**A:** So far, my joint projects have been fruitful and successful. I think they could be repeated with the same people. I believe the benefits outweigh the problems. You have two or more minds bringing solutions to the problems. The downside is coping with not offending your co-workers, as egos are involved. If it's a 50:50 clear collaboration, then it's a question of hammering it out, otherwise you need to be careful with issues of ownership and acknowledgement.

**Q:** With whom would you most like to collaborate?
**A:** The guys who built the Callanish monuments out on North Uist, but they're not around anymore, so I would settle for Bill Viola or Anselm Kiefer. They're the most interesting contemporary artists.

**Q:** Do you have a favourite work, or collection?
**A:** My first construction piece. It was a little blue box I made in memory of my father. I bitterly regret selling it to the Dundee Art Gallery and wish I still had it. Still, when you're younger and starting out and somebody wants to buy something you've made… More generally though, I really like one or two pieces from each stage of my work – mainly just for sentiment. For example, there's a picture I did of smokehouses in Arbroath that I love for just that reason.

**Q:** What sort of material do you see yourself producing say, five years from now?
**A:** No idea. Not a clue. *Driftworks* took two and a half years to put together and it was fairly risky. I'm just recovering from it, so I'm working on ongoing things and tying up loose ends. Until *Driftworks* has drifted out of my consciousness and something else has drifted in….

**Freya Reinsch** was born in Fresno, CA in 1979. She later moved to Los Angeles where she received her B.A. in English from UCLA. A year abroad in the UK inspired her to abandon a working life of certain misery in the Los Angeles film industry and relocate to St. Andrews. Freya would like to thank her parents for all their support and also to apologize in advance in case they inadvertently get the impression that parts of *Domestic* are based on their relationship. Lastly, in 1984, a baby boy came along and ruined Freya's young life as an only child. Today, that ratfaced little brother is one of the best things in her life. So, Chuck, this story is for you.

## FREYA REINSCH

# Domestic

EVERY SUNDAY, Mrs. Blackwood allowed herself to sleep in as late as she liked. Exhausted by the long week of keeping her splendid home in picture-perfect order, Sunday was her day to reward herself for her labors. It was usually noontime before she emerged from her white nest of bedclothes and rubbed the crust of sleep from the corners of her eyes (sleepy-bugs she'd called them, a lifetime ago when she was young). Sunlight beamed through the windows, hung against a marvelous wet-blue sky that pooled overhead like a watercolor sea. Mrs. Blackwood pulled the wrinkled sheets taut over the mattress, fluffed air into her crumpled feather pillows and straightened the luxurious duvet until it spilled across the bed like a silky length of bridal satin. After a reviving shower, Mrs. Blackwood slid a white slipdress over her head and went down the hall to look in on Baby's room.

Before venturing downstairs for breakfast Mrs. Blackwood always looked in on Baby's room, for at this hour he would have been in the middle of his morning nap. She eased the door open, careful not to make a sound, and poked her head into the cheery yellow-painted room. With the curtains tightly drawn as they always were, the light was heavy with a sobriety that belied the pleasant atmosphere. A subtle draught from the movement of the door stirred a small current in the air, disturbing the mobile of colorful zoo animals that hung over the crib into a trembling half-dance. Mrs. Blackwood eased back into the hallway, closing the door gently behind her. She considered for a moment whether or not she should continue to preserve the room, unused as it was, and then swiftly filed the thought in the part of her head reserved for Things She Mustn't Think About.

Floating down the slippery staircase in her airy linen dress, Mrs. Blackwood stepped carefully, for the blondwood had been resurfaced just that week and was still slick with fresh polish. In the vestibule, she tugged open the heavy oak front door and breezed over the threshold into the steamy afternoon to collect her Sunday newspaper. A well-groomed and expensive-looking marmalade cat sprawled lazily on the neat square of lawn. He was overweight and his appearance was not unlike that of an orange balloon animal, the sort that clowns twist together at children's birthday parties. Motes of sunlight caught in the inflated creature's glossy fur until it gleamed like a cloak of gold. Mrs. Blackwood smiled at her silly old lump of a cat as she scooped up the newspaper, the newsprint slightly runny from lying in the sun for several hours. Black type smeared onto the unblemished white skin of her right hand. Beyond her front yard, the street was a pleasant commotion of noise and activity. Children sailed back and forth on shiny bicycles, multicolored plastic streamers rippling from their handlebars, bicycle bells tinkling in harmony with their silvery childish laughter. Housewives sipped iced tea and chatted over fences in neighborly twos and threes while their husbands watered bushes of prizewinning roses, camellias and rhododendrons. Not one house looked significantly different from those on either side of it. Only the tiniest of details reminded Mrs. Blackwood who lived where and kept the street from blurring into an unbroken line of white picket fence, green lawn, white stucco and brown shingle. The Merriweathers had a cream-colored Chevrolet with gold detailing parked in their driveway. Two luminous pink plastic flamingoes lived on the Gayhearts' front lawn. The Honeywells' shingled roof boasted a brand-new satellite television dish.

The line of almost-identical houses was most noticeably interrupted by Mrs. Blackwood's own home. In place of the customary fence, her property was enclosed by an artfully pruned box hedge. As this particular feature of the Blackwoods' yard digressed somewhat radically from the general design of the neighborhood, it was a frequent topic of back-fence conversation among housewives who insistently fixated on the Blackwoods' heathen landscaping. Mrs. Blackwood hated the hedge. Her husband had insisted on having it and she silently begrudged the trouble it caused her on a daily basis.

With her unstained hand, Mrs. Blackwood waved sociably at several of her neighbors before turning back into the cool comfort of her home to prepare breakfast.

Mrs. Blackwood kept an especially lovely kitchen and delighted in each meal she took there. Every Sunday, she arrayed an attractive selection of food on a polished silver tray; one pink smile of cantaloupe, a small heap of red strawberries (green tops removed), two flaky croissants from the French bakery, a generous daub of raspberry jam and one steaming cup of peppermint tea. The tray was placed on the white-painted table, alongside the tidy spread of Sunday papers. Mrs. Blackwood glanced briefly at the front-page pictures and headlines before discarding them in favor of the entertainment section and its horoscopes, crossword and advice columns. A wedge of sunlight fell across her back, gently stroking her skin with its warmth and saturating the room with a soft vanilla glow. Sleek, white-tiled countertops glinted merrily as light glanced off their spotless surfaces. Slender fixtures of stainless steel gleamed like polished hematite. Clear vases of exquisite etched crystal held long-stemmed red roses in every corner, freshly cut from Mrs. Blackwood's very own garden. Against the pristine shiny-whiteness of Mrs. Blackwood's kitchen, these red roses stood out as clearly as blood on snow.

As a young girl, tasteful interior decorating magazines had consumed Mrs. Blackwood's imagination. Her kitchen, and the rest of the house for that matter, was arranged in the immaculate, photogenic style of the fashionable rooms that graced the glossy pages of such publications as *Sunset*, *Elle Décor*, and, of course, *Better Homes and Gardens*. Her mother received regular copies in the post and would pass them on to her fascinated daughter whose eyes shone with an insatiable appetite for images of the fairy-tales-come-true displayed between their attractive covers. Mrs. Blackwood had liked nothing better than to clasp a strand of smooth, white pearls around her neck, slide her small feet into a pair of her mother's high heels and sit in the porch swing with their shiny leather tips peeking out from beneath the ruffled hem of her best dress. Hours slipped away as easily as flour through a sieve as she pored through articles about wraparound sofas and bathroom motifs, all illustrated with photographs of fashionable housewives showcasing their own magazine-worthy homes for the enjoyment of the reading public. Mansions, country cottages and everything in between were built and filled with beautiful furniture arrangements inspired by these enchanting photo-stories within the realm of Mrs. Blackwood's young imagination. Now, in her late thirties, that dreamy little girl still lived somewhere inside Mrs. Blackwood and she was delighted to think that she very nearly lived in one of those magazine pages come to life.

Before she and her husband had moved into the house, it actually had been photographed for *Better Homes and Gardens* (a point of sale not overlooked by the Estate Agent). The purpose of the article was to showcase the heavy wooden beams that spanned the dramatic living-room ceiling. The official story was that these beams had been salvaged from a ruined church in Granada during the Spanish Civil War and shipped overseas at great expense by the house's original owner. To Mrs. Blackwood, those beams looked like any other slab of polished oak, but the story behind them and the fact that they had been featured in her favorite magazine made them seem mightily important.

Seated at her breakfast table, Mrs. Blackwood unfolded the entertainment section of her newspaper to the horoscope page. She first read her own (Sagittarius) and then her husband's (Gemini) and noted with pleasure that the astrologer had forecasted four-star days for the both of them. Yesterday had merely been a two-and-a-half star day for Mrs. Blackwood which was entirely true because she'd ruined a fresh manicure while driving home from the salon and then roasted a lemon and rosemary chicken to a dry crisp. She then carefully weighed the advice from Dear Abby to several disgruntled housewives and silently thanked God that she didn't have any problems serious enough to merit a letter to Dear Abby. Scanning the cinema listings, Mrs. Blackwood circled the showtimes for several new romantic comedies and wondered if her husband might like to go along and see one with her that week. One hour later, after finishing the enormous and dreadfully complicated Sunday crossword in record time, Mrs. Blackwood folded the newspaper neatly into its color-coded recycling bin (green for paper, brown for aluminum, black for glass) and cleared her dirty dishes from the table.

She stood at the sink and carefully passed each piece of tableware beneath the cool stream that poured from the swanlike faucet, soaping everything thoroughly to remove all traces of use. In spite of her care, a Royal Doulton teacup slipped from Mrs. Blackwood's soap-slippery fingers and nearly came to a shattering death in the basin. As she thrust her hand forward to rescue the expensive teacup, the too-large signet ring she wore around her thumb, fastened in place with a band of Scotch tape, slipped from her finger and disappeared down the drain in a whirlpool of water and suds.

Mrs. Blackwood gasped.

After a stunned, fatal pause in which the ring was lost forever, Mrs. Blackwood jammed her fingers down the drain but quickly understood that she was too late. The ring had dropped through the pipes and fallen into the City sewers by now, no doubt floating amongst all types of unspeakable refuse. Mrs. Blackwood mentally lashed herself for her carelessness.

Her husband had given her that ring ages ago, not long after they'd first met. They were students then and he didn't have enough money to buy her a new ring all for herself. He'd slid his signet, with its ornate, swirling 'B' for Blackwood, off his pinkie and onto the slender thumb of his future wife as they sunned themselves in the campus Quad one spring afternoon. Still too big for even her largest finger, the diminutive Mrs. Blackwood had always worn this token of affection beneath a generous wrapping of Scotch tape. She wondered for a moment where her husband kept his Kappa pledge pin, the one she'd given him after he made his gift of the signet. The one he always used to wear pinned to the waistband of his undershorts and swore he'd never take off as long as he lived. Mrs. Blackwood strained her memory but she couldn't recall noticing when the pin had first disappeared.

She remained motionless before the sink for some time, paralyzed by the silent reprimands that stormed through her head like an angry, insult-slinging hurricane. *You're stupid and careless*, she thought to herself. *You never deserved such a nice gift in the first place*. Twin tear-streams poured from corners of her eyes, traveling down mottled cheeks to gather at the overhang of her upper lip. Licking them away, Mrs. Blackwood's tongue was offended by the bitter, salty taste. Vanilla air clogged her throat until she thought she might choke. She leaned forward and wrenched open the windows, drawing the freshness of outside into her bursting lungs. Beneath the windowsill, a froth of red rosebushes blushed crimson against the white stucco wall of the house, the very same roses that provided new blooms for Mrs. Blackwood's crystal vases at least twice a week, roses which, on this miserable afternoon, gave Mrs. Blackwood not a bit of pleasure. Her teary eyes traveled across the lush grass, jeweltone flowerbeds and vivid greenery of her immaculate garden. A marble cherub urinated charmingly into a shallow, lily-strewn pond. Towards the back of the property, a cluster of apple trees huddled together intimately, red fruit spotting the foliage like rubies on green velvet. Mrs. Blackwood's eyes absently scanned all these attractive features before settling on the wall of box hedge at the rear of the garden. The whole of the nasty thing coiled around the perimeter of her yard like a leafy green snake.

*Maybe that just proves it's Eden*, Mrs. Blackwood consoled herself with a sigh. Any true Eden must have its snake, she supposed, and Mrs. Blackwood's existed in the form of that awful, constricting box hedge. No matter how much she tried to convince herself that the hedge existed for the purpose of authenticating her domestic paradise, she never stopped wishing the thing would just shrivel up and die.

The stooped, sweating figure of Mr. Blackwood could be seen pruning the top of the hedge. As loudly as Mrs. Blackwood had professed her hatred against the idea of installing that hedge, her husband had insisted upon it and finally got his way by simply coming home from work with a carload of hedge cuttings.

"But I want a fence," she'd moaned. "Everyone else on the street has a fence. Why do we have to be different?" Her pretty features wadded themselves into a scowl as she peered through the living-room window. An army of black plastic pots full of little green shrubs offended her front porch with their unwanted presence.

"Well, isn't that precisely why we should have something else?"

"I don't want something else! I want a fence and I want it painted white." Mrs. Blackwood folded her arms across her chest and sulked.

"Then our house will look exactly like all the others. Wouldn't you like to be a little different?" Her husband's tone was placating, as though he spoke to an excitable child.

"But we are different! Our driveway has a roadster. Everyone else's has a station wagon. Mrs. Honeywell asks me every day when we're going to get something family-sized."

"We'll get something family-sized once we've started a family. A hedge is going to look much nicer than a boring fence. I'll take care of it. You'll see." Mr. Blackwood had every intention of getting what he wanted. He had never known his wife to lift a finger in the direction of yardwork and hardly expected her to start with a project as big as enclosing the yard in a hedge or a fence. The house itself was her domain and he didn't see how there could be much of a fuss over keeping things that way.

Soon thereafter, a snake began to grow and thrive in her otherwise perfect garden. It grew slowly, leaves, centimeters, twigs and inches at a time, and the larger and greener it became, the tighter Mrs. Blackwood could feel it wrapping around her neck. One day, she thought, it might just crush her to death.

That afternoon, just like every other Sunday, Mr. Blackwood spent the day examining his box hedge with a ruler and leveling tool, making absolutely sure that every square inch of growth was precisely even with the square inch beside it. This was a highly methodical process that always took the whole of the day, much to Mrs. Blackwood's irritation. Her husband was a doctor who worked as much as sixty hours a week. Saturdays he used up with all the planting, weeding and mowing it took to maintain such a splendid garden as theirs was. Sunday was devoted entirely to the hedge. The goshdarn awful, stupid, cursed hedge. The hedge that coiled around her neck and kept her wrapped up inside herself and never ever let her out. The hedge that made them different and made their neighbors talk.

Mrs. Blackwood gathered all the willpower she could summon and used it to stuff a cork in the cloudy mood that lay bottled behind her eyes, shadowing her sunny day to a dreary charcoal gray. She leaned forward into the warm, butter-gold sunshine and called to her husband in her usual gay tone, "Hello out there! Would my darling like me to make him some fresh lemonade and a nice ham sandwich?"

Mr. Blackwood stood up and squinted in the direction of his wife's singsongy voice, sugarcoated to mask a frothing discontent. Shielding his eyes from the glare of the sun, he waved energetically before bending over the hedge again. Mrs. Blackwood observed with mounting frustration as he skimmed a microscopic growth from the inner wall of the hedge with the blade of his shears. "You spend so much time in that yard, I almost think you don't live here anymore!" she called, her voice as sweet and bubbly as pink champagne.

Mr. Blackwood waved again, but this time over his shoulder without even bothering to stand up. Mrs. Blackwood sighed and lowered the window.

Her lower lip quavered as her thoughts returned to the lost signet ring, imagining that by now it was probably lodged in the belly of a scum-coated sewer rat. Although she appeared outwardly composed, cool and creamy as a new bottle of milk, she was slick with icy pearls of sweat beneath her loose white dress. She felt the freezing drops of suppressed inner torment pool in the cleft between her breasts before dripping like melted icicles down her ribcage and across the fleshy skin of her abdomen. Mrs. Blackwood shivered like a frostbitten squirrel before the kitchen sink, still standing in her pie-slice of streaming sunlight. Her fingers went shakily to her wedding and engagement rings, still stacked atop one another on her fourth finger. They felt suddenly strange, almost foreign, without the signet to complete the trio of bands that she had always worn.

The elastic that had held the newspaper in its neat, fat roll still lay on the breakfast table. Mrs. Blackwood wrapped it around her naked thumb until the skin pinched, trying to recover the sensation of her husband's missing signet ring. Compared to the former beauty of the gold ring with its swirly engraving, the rubber band looked about as becoming on her finger as a withered gray worm.

It was very romantic how her husband had asked Mrs. Blackwood to marry him. They had been together throughout most of their University student days, meeting in the campus union just before Christmas of their freshman year. Mr. Blackwood had been reading in the lounge when his future wife blew through the swinging doors like a warm gust of late-summer wind. She took one look at the ridiculous Christmas tree that towered in the corner of the room, bedecked in school-pride ribbons of blue and gold, and burst out laughing. She had a rich, musky laugh and caramel features that made her instantly likeable. Although she was quickly shushed by an unimpressed student reading biochemistry, Mr. Blackwood liked her high spirits and resolved to speak with her as soon as he found the opportunity. He didn't have to wait long; she collapsed into the armchair beside him, stifling her giggles through one hand clapped across her mouth. Mr. Blackwood sneaked a conspiratorial smile at her over the rim of his anatomy book and the rest, as they say, was history.

Until graduation, anyway, at which point the relationship became history. Mr. Blackwood stayed on at the University for medical school. Future Mrs. Blackwood wished to see more of the world and accepted a one-year teaching position at an all-girls' school in Athens. They bid one another a tearful goodbye, promising to write whenever possible, to visit when time and money allowed, and to always leave their hearts and minds open to being together again in the future.

This lasted for two weeks.

Afraid he might lose Future Mrs. Blackwood if he didn't take action, Mr. Blackwood telegrammed Athens asking her to marry him. Future Mrs. Blackwood telegrammed right back to tell him, *No, you must ask in person.* Eighteen hours later, there was a knock on the door of her small flat above an olive merchant near the Acropolis. The whitewashed door swung open and there he was, already kneeling, a pear-shaped cubic zirconium ring trembling between his thumb and forefinger. She dropped to her knees in front of him, her face flushed with joy and tears, effusing *Yes yes yes!* before he'd even asked The Question again. Her arms flew around his neck and her soft pink mouth peppered his stubbly cheek with saltwater kisses. After some minutes of this emotional outpouring, he suggested they had better move inside.

A blissful year ensued during which Mr. Blackwood deferred his medical course to be with his fiancée in Greece. Most of their world in Athens revolved within the salty, pungent air of that small single room above the olive-seller. It was a modest room, with only a hot plate for cooking and a lumpy fold-out bed that doubled as a couch in the daytime. There was a valley running down the center of the mattress that always sent Future Mrs. Blackwood rolling into Mr. Blackwood's side during the night. She dug herself out of the mattress valley each morning at eight-thirty to teach English at the nearby girls' school. By one in the afternoon, she was back again and they would shower together to wash the sticky heat from their bodies and then spend the rest of the hot day in the apartment, cooling themselves by staying wrapped in damp towels. For dinner, they wandered through local markets, eating fresh olives and tomatoes rolled in hummus and stuffed into the bread-pocket of a pitta. Once, Mr. Blackwood ate ten servings of tripe in one meal because it was the cheapest food available and spent the next two days in the bathroom. He even had to send Future Mrs. Blackwood foraging in the bathrooms of nearby tourist hotels to replenish his supply of toilet paper. After he finished being sick, they joked about the incident often, laughing as they warned travelers in the Agora away from tripe vendors. They spent holidays on sailboats, circling white-village islands of dramatic red rock, set like lustrous jewels against a satiny cushion of blue sea. Their skin turned brown-red like the island sands from their afternoons in the sun and their hair, which they both wore in a similar close-cropped style, was bleached white as flax. From a distance, one could scarcely tell them apart.

In the summer, after Mrs. Blackwood finished her teaching duties, they left Athens and rented a sailboat which they lived on for three whole months. They ate, swam, made love and did little else. They were always hungry and often fished off the side of the boat, or docked at small villages to buy fruit and vegetables. As much and as often as they ate, they could never quite fill their stomachs and often started lunch just after finishing breakfast. Nearly always they would make love in between meals and then go for a quick swim in the Aegean, which would only make them hungrier. By the end of that wonderful summer, Mr. Blackwood and his future wife were so full of Greece, food and each other that they never imagined any of it could change.

They were sorry to say goodbye to Greece and the happy, listless warmth of their days there, but they had agreed to return home together after one year so that they could be married and so Mr. Blackwood could continue his medical degree. Within a week of their return, they stood in City Hall before a witness and were married in a civil ceremony. Mrs. Blackwood, who was quite fashionably unconventional in those days, wore a white eyelet minidress with knee-high boots of white patent leather. Mr. Blackwood wore a smart-looking pinstripe suit. Afterwards, they had a lunch of fried-egg sandwiches and drank coronas in a local diner and then went and had their picture taken in the Harbor, in front of the silver suspension Bridge, its heavy metal cords as graceful from a distance as the strings of an enormous harp. They looked like two fashionable young people on their way to a nice dinner, or two hipsters forced to scrub up for a Sunday outing with their parents. No one would ever be able to guess from the photograph that the young couple was newly married.

As she sifted through these happy old memories, Mrs. Blackwood was overtaken by a fabulous idea. While Mr. Blackwood spent his afternoon clipping away at his box hedge, she would prepare several dishes from their days in Greece for dinner. He would come in from his yardwork, tired, sweating and hungry, and find his doting wife at the dinner table with a Greek feast spread before her. Not only that, but Mrs. Blackwood planned to wait for her husband wearing no clothes! They hadn't had sex in several months - no, a year or perhaps longer. At least not since before Baby was born. Besides, he worked such unreasonable hours at the hospital that she was always asleep by the time he came home from work. Mrs. Blackwood inwardly congratulated herself for her ingenuity.

It was because of Baby that Mr. Blackwood had started sleeping in the guest bedroom. He came home from the Hospital late one evening to find his wife had fallen asleep in their bed with the newborn child curled against her. He showered before joining them between the crisp, white sheets, smiling as he thought of how close and cozy it would be to sleep with Baby in the middle. He had a shave after his shower, deciding that it would allow him to sleep a little later the next morning. The flat, white surface of his palm swirled circles in the clouded mirror, leaving streaks in the glass that would make Mrs. Blackwood frown in the morning. He hummed softly to himself as he scraped stubble from his cheeks through a puff of white shaving foam. After a swift rinse that didn't fully clear the sink of foam splatters or short, thorny hairs, Mr. Blackwood tiptoed back into the bedroom. Moonlight slanted in through the open window, silvering the white bedclothes until they gleamed like precious metal. His wife's hair, longer now, and a rich chocolate color from a recent trip to the hairdresser's, streamed like fudge syrup across the white feather pillow. Her arm curved protectively around Baby, pulling him close to her breast. Mr. Blackwood thought they looked like the very picture of warmth and serenity. He slipped happily between the sweet-smelling sheets and nestled close beside his sleeping wife and child.

Instantly, Baby began to cry.

He wouldn't stop crying, even after hours of cooing and rocking and walking around the room. They tried feeding him, burping him, changing his diaper, even playing soft music. Nothing made any difference; his screams intensified and his poor, hysterical face grew as red and splotchy as a boiled new potato. He began to hiccup and continued to cry so hard that his entire body shook. He cried so hard that he began to have trouble breathing. Mr. Blackwood felt especially helpless and finally had to move down the hall to sleep in the guest bedroom as he was expected back at the Hospital early the next morning. A few short minutes after settling himself into the cold, unused guest bed, the crying stopped.

The same scenario was repeated the very next night.

On the fifth night, Mr. Blackwood came home from the Hospital and went defeatedly into the guest bedroom after seeing his wife asleep with Baby yet again. The pair of them scarcely ever argued, but that Sunday as they sat together in the kitchen over breakfast, Mr. Blackwood had a few grievances to air.

"I think it's time Baby learned to sleep in his crib." His words dropped onto the kitchen table like a rain of cold, hard stones. Mrs. Blackwood instantly stiffened.

"I don't see what's wrong with him staying in our bed." She avoided her husband's eye as she spooned cream-of-wheat into her mouth, concentrating on the pool of brown sugar that dissolved on her tongue.

"Well, for one thing, he won't let me sleep there. Or hadn't you noticed? He screams and cries whenever I try to get in bed with you." His wife's inattention bothered him, so Mr. Blackwood removed the breakfast spoon from her hand and forced her to look at him.

Mrs. Blackwood stared meaningfully at her husband with her wide, blue eyes. "It gets lonely at night when you come home so late from work. I feel better if I can have Baby next to me. I don't want to put him in his crib." Her mouth drooped into a pout and her voice was punctuated with the threat of tears.

Mr. Blackwood didn't know what to say about his hours at work. Nothing could be done about that. He had a living to earn and a family to provide for. He also hated that his wife cried anytime he tried to argue with her. She was impossible to talk to when she was crying. "Well, I don't like it," he muttered, "and I don't think it's safe."

"How's that?" The blue eyes widened. They looked like rainwater puddles that had caught the reflection of new blue sky after a violent storm.

"He's so tiny. You might roll on top of him in the middle of the night. He couldn't breathe like that. What if you didn't wake up in time?"

Her pale brow wrinkled as she thought for a minute. The blue puddle-eyes narrowed to defiant slits. "I could never hurt him. He'll stay with me if I want him to. I'm not lonely when I've got Baby."

After that, Mr. Blackwood retreated permanently to the solitude of the guest bedroom.

With the kitchen as clean as if it had never been used, Mrs. Blackwood headed back upstairs to coat her toenails with glittery red varnish (another Sunday ritual). On her way, she opened the front door again to see if the cat might like to come inside. As the afternoon heat had intensified, he now took refuge beneath the white Mercedes station wagon that sat majestically in the driveway (the sporty roadster had been replaced when Baby was born). Although she called and gestured invitingly, the cat ignored Mrs. Blackwood. He did not even open his eyes to look at her, but merely twitched his ears in the direction of her voice as he remained, otherwise immobile, in the cool shade beneath the car. *Drat, you mean old cat. You awful, ungrateful old thing,* Mrs. Blackwood hissed inside her head as she slammed the heavy door shut behind her. The loud crash made her wince and she looked up guiltily towards Baby's room. She glided soundlessly back up the slippery blondwood stairs and poked her head into the yellow room for the second time that day; it was as silent and still as before. She closed the door again with a sigh.

In her own bedroom, Mrs. Blackwood stood in front of the full-length mirror, balls of cotton stuffed between her newly-varnished toes, and pulled her white dress off over her head. After stepping out of her white cotton underwear, she was fully naked before her own reflection. She was displeased by what she saw, glaring with disapproval at her fleshy stomach and sagging breasts. Bruise-colored stretch marks streaked across her abdomen, thighs and buttocks like swipes from a careless purple crayon. Although she was still fairly young, giving birth nearly a year ago had certainly taken its toll on Mrs. Blackwood's once-firm body. She hated exercise. Sweating disgusted her and the smell of locker rooms made her nauseous. She used to go out for walks, pushing Baby ahead of her with a towel draped over his stroller to keep out the sun's burning rays. With Baby gone, she didn't take those walks anymore. Besides, it was scorching outside and the intense sunlight might liver-spot her skin.

Standing sideways, Mrs. Blackwood noted with distaste that her stomach resembled a fat, drooping bead of sap oozing slowly down the trunk of a wrinkled tree. She straightened her spine, sucked in her stomach, clenched her jaw to tighten the loose skin at her throat, and wondered to herself how such a sight would ever appeal to her husband over dinner that night. She gave her stomach a few mean pinches that left stinging pink half-moons from the filed tips of her fingernails, a punishment for eating so much and for turning into such a fat goose. She wrapped herself glumly in a soft white robe instead of the dress she'd worn earlier and thought she'd better go downstairs to get dinner started.

Mrs. Blackwood paused at the top of the stairwell and looked down the hall at the closed door of Baby's room. She decided she could allow herself one, just one, more look for today. Poised on the threshold of the little room, yellow as a field of spring daffodils inside, Mrs. Blackwood pressed her ear gently to the door and listened for any sound from within. Hearing nothing, she twisted the cool brass knob until the door gave way and swung slowly open, grazing the thick pile carpet as it traveled. Barefoot, Mrs. Blackwood stepped into the quiet light and padded across the soft floor towards the crib.

The fresh disturbance in the air had shaken the zoo animals into their bouncing half-dance again. The toy shelf became a set of teddy bear bleachers as rows of stuffed animals with glinting, black-button eyes seemed to follow Mrs. Blackwood's tiptoeing movements like a crowd of voiceless spectators. In a corner, an antique rocking-horse with soulful eyes like two black pools gazed at her with a sad understanding. A perfect tower of blondwood building blocks sat atop the yellow chest of drawers. Everything was in spotless order and not a mote of dust could be seen lurking in any of the muted corners.

Brown Bear, the baby's favorite stuffed toy, was tucked into the crib where Baby himself would have slept. His furry head rested on the tiny white pillow and the pink receiving blanket was tucked neatly around his plush body, almost the same size Baby had been when…

Mrs. Blackwood's composure collapsed before that sentence could finish itself.

Moist hands as pale and fishy as raw oysters flew to her throat as if to struggle against an invisible assailant and she began to feel as though she might choke. The air in the room turned thick and suffocating – perhaps coming in here hadn't been such a good idea after all – and, breathing in rapid, desperate bursts of air, she thrust her arm down into the crib and yanked Brown Bear from his carefully made bed. A cold tiara of sweat-crystals ringed her clammy forehead. With the bear in her arms, Mrs. Blackwood stumbled backwards from the crib as though she'd been pushed, crashing into the block-tower as she tried to recover her footing. There was an enormous clatter as the structure toppled from the collision, blocks raining down all over the springy carpet. Gasping for breath, Mrs. Blackwood fled the room for the safety of the hallway.

She no longer felt she could prepare dinner, returning instead to her bedroom where she could telephone a nearby Greek restaurant for delivery. After placing her order, she climbed back into her soft, white bed and pulled Brown Bear to her breast. With tears staining the pillow beneath her cheek, Mrs. Blackwood slept until the sound of the doorbell woke her at dusk.

Mrs. Blackwood stood at the white kitchen counter, spooning the contents of several white take-out cartons into attractive china bowls. There was a Greek salad with crisp red bell peppers, cherry tomatoes, and crumbly white chunks of feta cheese sequined with a generous sprinkling of kalamata olives. Vine leaves, oozing fresh olive oil, were arranged in a pretty, spiralling pattern on the china serving plate. The pitta bread-pockets and strips of grilled chicken were placed in the oven to keep warm until dinnertime while the baklava remained in its ribboned pastry box as a surprise for dessert. Mrs. Blackwood carried the cold items into the dining room where the rosewood table had already been laid with her finest silver dinnerware. An etched-crystal vase held a fresh arrangement of red roses from the garden. Scented candlesticks rose gracefully from silver pillars on either side of the vase. The dishes were placed neatly beside the roses, and a thin sheet of cling film was laid over the salad to prevent the lettuce leaves from wilting in the warm air.

Mr. Blackwood would be inside in not more than half an hour and everything was nearly perfect.

Back in the kitchen, Mrs. Blackwood searched for her husband through the window above the kitchen sink. Her eyes finally found him crouched beside the hedge towards the rear of the garden, not much farther down from where she'd seen him early that afternoon. A foul taste crept into her mouth as she watched Mr. Blackwood hold his yardstick vertically against the wall of the hedge and move it slowly, one tiny inch at a time, down a portion of its length. Every foot or so, he would pause to shave an invisible stray growth from the top of the hedge with his clippers. It had taken two and a half years to grow to a height of precisely one yard and Mr. Blackwood was obsessed with maintaining that exact level. Mrs. Blackwood couldn't for the life of her understand why the hedge was worth the amount of time and work required for its upkeep. A fence would have been much more practical. Sighing, she removed two goblets from the cupboard and carried them, along with a bottle of retsina, into the dining room. Dusk was falling like swift silence and when the light went, Mr. Blackwood would have to come inside. His wife would be ready.

The chicken and oven-warmed pittas joined the salad, hummus and vine leaves on the dining room table. With no preparations left, Mrs. Blackwood had nothing to do but discard her robe and wait for her husband in one of the velvet-cushioned chairs. She draped her white robe loosely over the seatback and lowered herself onto the soft padding. With some distaste, she noted the way her stomach bulged and folded about her midsection like raw pastry dough as she sat. She removed the robe from the chair and drew it across her lap; that was better. Goose flesh had started to prickle her arms and breasts. With the sun now dipping far below the trees, the warmth in the air had vanished, giving way to a faint chill that made Mrs. Blackwood's nakedness not altogether comfortable. She wished her husband would hurry. Dinner grew cold as she shifted around in her chair. Feeling as though she might cry again, Mrs. Blackwood pressed her teeth into her lower lip to stifle any tears. It was fully dark outside now. Where was her husband?

Finally, the back door slammed.

Swallowing what felt like a jagged rock in her throat, Mrs. Blackwood called brightly, "Honey, in here!"

Seconds later, Mr. Blackwood's sweaty figure appeared in the doorframe. A grimy, dirt-streaked towel hung around his shoulders and he sopped his dripping brow with one sodden corner. He couldn't quite make out his wife's nude figure in the semi-darkness.

"What are you doing sitting in the dining room with no lights on?"

"I thought we could have a nice dinner together. I've ordered Greek." Pink champagne bubbles burst faintly on her tongue; only a few of them now made their way into the open air with the rest of her voice

"Oh." Mr. Blackwood buried his entire face in the towel and rubbed vigorously.

"Darling, come sit down. Aren't you hungry? You've been working so hard!"

"Not really. I've been eating apples from the orchard all day. And just an hour ago, Mrs. Gayheart passed me a slice of blackberry pie over her back fence."

Mrs. Blackwood ignored the painful stab of her husband's disinterest and picked up the book of matches that sat by her napkin. There was a brief streak of flame and a nose-tickling smell of sulphur as she touched a lit match to each of the candles that stood stiff and erect on either side of the rose bouquet. "But I've ordered all of our favorite old foods! Do come sit down." She fidgeted as her husband looked at her strangely, noticing her nakedness for the first time in the flickering sepia light of the candle-flames.

"How long have you been sitting there like that?"

"Not long. I've just been waiting for you." She cast her eyes downward, unable to meet her husband's confused expression. In the half-light, her dark, heavy eyelids seemed hooded with wrinkled eggplant skins.

"You should put some clothes on. It will be cooler tonight and you don't want to catch a cold."

"I thought this would be a nice surprise. It's been quite a long time…" Mrs. Blackwood lifted the robe from her lap and drew it tightly around her shoulders.

Her husband paused, scratched his head and opened his mouth to speak. He shut it again and everything was silent for what felt like several minutes. Finally, he managed to push a few words past his unwilling lips. "Whatever you don't eat, leave in the fridge. I'll take it with me in the morning. You'll remember that I have to be away all week at the Pediatrics Conference."

"Yes, I remember," his wife whispered miserably. She was drawn into as tight a ball as she could manage while seated in the chair. "You'd better have a shower and get packed. I'll wrap something up for you to take with you."

Mr. Blackwood let the towel fall around his shoulders again. His blond hair, damp with sweat and darkened by dirt looked almost earth-colored in the dusky light. Mrs. Blackwood heard the steady tread of his footfalls as he turned down the hallway and then ascended the wooden staircase. A few moments later, she could hear him directly overhead as he moved about his own bedroom, pulling open drawers and turning on the water in the shower. A thin, high-pitched hiss burst from the pipes as the water heated and began to flow. Mrs. Blackwood rose from her chair and knotted her robe around her waist so firmly that she nearly couldn't breathe before clearing the table of the unused dishes and uneaten food.

When Mrs. Blackwood rubbed the crust of sleep from her eyes the next morning, cheerful sunlight filled her bedroom with a naïve yellow glow. The sky was as blue and the colors of her garden as vivid as they had been the morning before. Everything sparkled once again with optimism, as though all of the previous day's unpleasantness was no more real than a bad dream. Mrs. Blackwood roused herself drowsily from the tangled bedclothes and began to remake the bed, spreading out the wrinkles with her palms until the topsheet was as smooth as a flat, white stone. Brown Bear emerged from beneath a smothering mass of white feather pillows where he'd presumably been shoved by Mrs. Blackwood in her sleep. She polished his black-button eyes with the hem of her nightgown and sat him on the windowsill to enjoy the morning sun. Out front, the driveway was empty; Mr. Blackwood had already left and wouldn't return until the following Friday night.

Mrs. Blackwood went to her nightstand and removed the telephone directory from the drawer. After thumbing through the white and yellow pages to a section that had been bookmarked for some time, Mrs. Blackwood found the number she was searching for: Landscape Architect.

Five days later, after witnessing with great satisfaction the leafy carnage that was the death of her husband's perfect hedge, Mrs. Blackwood stood in her front yard and inspected the new fence that now enclosed the property. Its splendid coat of fresh white paint glistened exquisitely in the bright afternoon sun. It was hours until Mr. Blackwood was expected home and Mrs. Blackwood intended to spend every daylight minute of that time luxuriating in her re-designed landscape. Now we're just like everyone else, she thought to herself, a beatific smile spreading across her pale face. She inhaled deeply and relished the disappearance of the imaginary snake she could no longer feel wrapped around her neck, choking her breath. Glancing at an upstairs window, that of her bedroom, Mrs. Blackwood caught the beady black gaze of Brown Bear. His red embroidered mouth smiled down at her in an eternal expression of complicit reassurance. Mrs. Blackwood folded her arms across the flour-streaked front of her white apron and positively radiated with pleasure.

The new front gate creaked open, interrupting Mrs. Blackwood's happy reverie. The Mailman had arrived with an armful of catalogs and envelopes to deposit on the Blackwood front porch.

"Oh, just hand them right to me!" Mrs. Blackwood chirped. "There isn't anything to collect today anyway." The Mailman transferred his load into Mrs. Blackwood's outstretched arms.

"There you go, Ma'am," he replied, tipping his hat amicably. "Yard looks nice," he added, scanning the garden as he wiped a thin film of sweat from his steaming brow.

"Oh why thank you! I can't wait until my husband sees it." Mrs. Blackwood smiled broadly at the Mailman. "He's been out of town all this past week," she continued, lowering her voice to a confiding hush.

"Looks spectacular. He'll be impressed! You have a good one, Ma'am and I'll just be on my way now." The gate clicked shut behind the Mailman's retreating figure. The sharp, satisfying click of new, well-oiled metal was so musical to Mrs. Blackwood's ears that she didn't even hear the Mailman's buoyant whistling as he moved along the sidewalk towards the next house.

Mrs. Blackwood clasped the pile of mail to her chest and retreated into the shade of the front steps. Perching delicately on the topmost step, Mrs. Blackwood sifted through the heap of magazines, letters, coupons and mail-order catalogs the Mailman had brought that day. The expensive-looking marmalade cat emerged from a patch of ivy beneath the dining room window and began to purr rapturously as he wove himself around Mrs. Blackwood's legs. Tufts of orange cat hair clung to the white hem of her dressing gown, beneath which the fuzzy, rounded toes of two pink house slippers peeked bashfully. Arriving at the bottom of the heap of mail, Mrs. Blackwood came upon the newest issue of *Better Homes and Gardens*. She marveled at the cover photograph which depicted a miniaturized replica of a medieval castle, only smaller, newer and modern. 'Living A Fairy-Tale' sang the tall white letters that scrolled across the shining cover; 'A Castle Home to Match Your Dreams'. Mrs. Blackwood, glanced up from the magazine to have another look at her gleaming white fence, shinier than mother-of-pearl with its coat of fresh paint. It was the final missing piece to her own dream home and now that it was in place, there was nothing further to wish for. Everything felt complete.

All up and down the street, charming rows of identical houses sat behind identical white fences. Several husbands pushed lawn mowers back and forth across tidy squares of green grass while their wives plucked long stems of pink and red roses from beautifully pruned bushes, their hair tucked beneath attractive silky scarves to protect from the sun. The neighborhood children coasted up and down the street on bicycles as the tinkle of their laughter mingled with the silvery tones of the bicycle bells. Mrs. Blackwood smiled at the idyllic scene that spread before her, traveling down both sides of the street as far as her squinting eyes could see. Sighing with contentment, she returned her attention to the magazine in her lap and blissfully immersed herself in the sugared words and candied images of the front-page article.

**Emma Parfitt** was born on 28 August, 1979, Wrexham, Wales. She has lived in seven different places since then (Oban, Dalmally, Blackpool, Redditch, Ballater, Edinburgh, and St Andrews). Came here to study Science, then chucked it in to become a writer. Now lives in a mysterious place, not unlike Durably, but with a chip shop. And is an international Invisible Snooker Champion in her spare time.

EMMA PARFITT

# How The Herring Became a Kipper

THERE ONCE was a man called Benjamin who lived, with his wife Nancy, in a little hut on a hill overlooking the sea. One day Benjamin fell ill and could not eat. No matter what his wife tried to tempt him with, Benjamin shook his head and said, "I am not hungry."

Nancy tried her best. But every day when she made him his breakfast, even though his stomach was rumbling, he said, "I am not hungry," and pushed his plate away.

Finally Nancy had had enough and decided to find out why her husband would not eat. "What did you do on the day you fell ill?" she asked.

Benjamin scratched his head. "I went to paint a house on the beach."

So Nancy put on her shoes and her coat, and walked down the hill to the beach to see what had made her husband refuse to eat any of the food she made for him.

She knocked on the door of the house, and waited for an answer. She knocked again. No one replied. Then she saw that her husband had left his ladder leaning against the side of the building, next to a large window.

Carefully, Nancy climbed the ladder and looked in. The whole room was filled, from floor to ceiling, with fish tanks. There were big tanks, small tanks, square tanks, round tanks, and triangular tanks all around the walls. And inside the tanks were dozens of different kinds of fish. There were red fish, blue fish, big fish, little fish, striped fish, spotty fish, every kind of fish in the world.

"What is this?" Nancy said to herself. "Perhaps he saw all the fish while he was working, and they looked so nice, and he was so hungry that all he wanted to eat was fish. Could that be it?"

So Nancy went to the market and bought one of every fish she could find. She took them all home, and presented them to her husband.

He looked at the fish, and said, "I am not hungry."

Now Nancy did not notice the cat purring around her ankles. She did not know what she was going to do with all the fish she had bought at the market. But what worried her most was how she was going to get her husband to eat again. There must have been something she missed at the house that would show her what to do.

So Nancy picked up her coat, put on her shoes, and walked all the way back down the hill to the beach. She climbed up the ladder once more, and looked in the window. Nancy saw everything that she had seen before. Big tanks, small tanks, square tanks, round tanks, triangular tanks stood around the walls. Red fish, blue fish, big fish, little fish, striped fish, spotty fish, every kind of fish in the world. But then she noticed that the tank under the window was empty.

"Aha!" Nancy said. "I wonder if this tank held the fish my husband saw, and found so tasty he will not eat anything else. Who could tell me if he ate the fish that swam in that tank?"

As she pondered what to do next, a bespectacled little man walked up the front steps and let himself in.

Nancy climbed down off the ladder, and knocked on the door.

"Come in," the little man said. So she went into the room she had seen through the window. Around her she could see big tanks, small tanks, square tanks, round tanks, triangular tanks all around the walls; and red fish, blue fish, big fish, little fish, striped fish, spotty fish, every kind of fish in the world. And an empty tank under the window.

"Ah, I see you are wondering why this tank is empty," said the little old man. His eyes looked like lakes through his glasses. "One day this tank will hold the herring. It will be the tastiest fish ever. All you will ever want to eat is this kind of fish... It is a marvellous fish."

"I am the painter's wife," Nancy said. "Did you tell my husband about this marvellous herring of yours?"

"Yes, yes I did. He asked me why this tank was empty, and I told him that one day this tank will hold the herring. It will be the tastiest fish ever. All he will ever want to eat will be this kind of fish... It is a marvellous fish."

Nancy knew that her husband, a very sincere man, was foolish enough to believe what the bespectacled little man had told her about the herring.

"Now that you have told him this," said Nancy, "my husband will not eat." She was very angry. "Where is this fish that you talk about? My husband will not eat anything but this fish, and will starve if I do not get it for him."

"Oh, dear," said the man. "This is unfortunate."

"Where is the fish?" Nancy said again, pointing to the tank.

"This fish has not been made yet."

"Not been made?"

"I am a fish expert. I travel the world in search of new fish. As you can see, I am so good at my job that I have them all. Upset that I had run out of work I went to see the Fishmaker responsible for making new fish for me to find. Down to the bottom of the sea I went, from the blue clear water of the beach to the darkness far below, until I reached the great sea trench where the Fishmaker lives, surrounded by hot volcanic vents.

"I stood before the Fishmaker, and he asked me, 'What do you want, Fishfinder?'

"'There are no more fish for me to find,' I told him. 'You are not making fish fast enough.'

"'But I am working on one now,' he said. 'It will be the nicest fish you have ever tasted. No one will want to eat any other fish but this. It is a marvellous fish. But making things takes time. If you want me to do it right then you must leave me alone to get on with my work. You shall know it when you see it. It shall be called the herring.'"

"I was so excited that I came home as fast as I could. And made a tank for the fish out of the best materials I could find. I asked your husband to paint my house a nice bright colour, because when people hear of this fish they will come from far-off lands to see it. Then your husband asked about the fish, and I told him what I have told you."

Nancy wrung her hands. "My husband will soon starve if he does not eat. How long ago did you see the Fishmaker?"

"Weeks and weeks ago," said the man. "I could take you to see him so you can tell him about your husband."

"Thank you," she said.

So the Fishfinder took Nancy down to the bottom of the sea, from the clear blue water of the land to the darkness of the trench below, where the Fishmaker lives surrounded by hot volcanic vents. Nancy was awed by the size and beauty of his underwater home. Around its green courtyard swam thousands of colourful fish. The Fishfinder led her through the courtyard to a huge room, where a green man sat on a coral throne, wearing a crown of fish fins.

"Hello Fishfinder," said the Fishmaker. "Who is this?"

"This is the painter's wife. I told the painter of your herring, and he will not eat anything else until he has tried one."

"Ah, my wonderful herring," said the sad Fishmaker. "It has all gone wrong."

"Then what am I to do?" cried Nancy. "My husband will starve. Why did you say you could make such a marvellous fish if you could not?"

"Oh, I made the fish all right," said the Fishmaker. "But the Fishfinder was so busy making his tank for my new fish, he forgot to find and name it."

"That can be easily fixed," said the Fishfinder. "Tell me where the fish is, and I shall name it at once."

"Yes, yes," said Nancy. "Name it at once."

"Too late," said the Fishmaker. "They found it, and named it tuna."

"Tuna!" cried Nancy. "But my husband wants herring. I have to give him a herring, or he shall starve."

"Here," said the Fishmaker. "Take this fish. The Fishfinder can name it a herring, and your husband will not starve." He handed her his new creation. "It does not look or taste as nice as my original herring. But he will like it."

"Thank you," said Nancy.

Quickly the Fishfinder named the fish a herring. Then up they went, away from the colourful fish in the dark water below, to the clear water above where the Fishfinder's house stood on the beach.

Nancy thanked the Fishfinder, and brought the herring to her husband.

"Here is your herring, Husband," Nancy said. "I will cook it for you at once."

Nancy put the herring on a large plate, and picked up a knife to slice it open.

"Wait. I just remembered, there is no lemon for the fish. You can't have fish without lemon. I shall go to the market and buy one. Watch the fish, and make sure that the cat doesn't get it."

Benjamin sat with the herring before him. Except for the cat, and the fish, he was alone in the hut. And the fish smelt good.

Now Benjamin had not eaten for a long time. Nor had he slept for thoughts of this marvellous fish. After a little while his eyes began to close. Just as he was drifting off to sleep, the cat jumped up on the table and tried to grab the herring. Benjamin pushed it away.

"Bad cat! This fish is not for you," Benjamin said. He looked about for somewhere safe to put the herring until his wife returned. But there was nowhere to put the plate where the cat could not reach it. Then Benjamin looked at the washing line strung across the room. Could he hang the fish there? Why not? Benjamin took a clothes peg, and hung the herring from the washing line by its tail. He stood at the door of the hut, and waited for Nancy's return.

"How long will she take?" he said, glancing at the fish.

The sky began to get a little darker as the sun went down.

"Nancy will be home soon, and we will be able to cook the fish," said Benjamin. He decided to light a fire, so that when she returned everything would be ready. He piled a heap of wood in the fireplace, and lit it. The cat got in his way as it prowled beneath the washing line, and looked up at the fish with two alert green eyes. He pushed it outside.

"Go away cat."

The sky darkened further. Benjamin's fire filled the room with its warmth. It was too warm. Benjamin walked outside into the green garden that looked out over the sea. Then he heard a cry from the road. "Benjamin!" It was his friend Simon.

"Hello, Simon."

"Could you help me? My arms are sore from carrying my bags up the hill."

"Did you see Nancy on your way up?" Benjamin said.

"Yes. She said she was hoping to get a lemon before the market closed."

Benjamin helped Simon to carry all the things he had bought to a house on the other side of the hill.

Meanwhile, inside Benjamin's hut, the cat was still trying to reach the fish. It leaped, claws outstretched, missed the herring and landed with a paw in the fire. Benjamin's chair was set alight beneath the fish as the logs rolled to the kitchen floor. As the cat ran away limping wisps of woody smoke began to drift up towards the ceiling, and out of the window.

Nancy saw the smoke on her return, and rushed in thinking that the house was on fire. There she found a heap of wood burning on the floor. And the herring she had gone to so much trouble to get, hung above it on the washing line. Nancy threw water over the burning chair, and put the fish back on its plate. When Benjamin got home she was very upset.

"Where have you been? I returned home to find the kitchen on fire. And the herring hung on the washing line."

"I was tired and hungry. I hung up the fish to keep it safe from the cat, and lit a fire for your return."

"But why make a fire on the kitchen floor?" said Nancy.

As she spoke the cat limped back into the kitchen.

"Now I know what happened," said Benjamin. "The cat knocked the logs out of the fireplace, trying to get the herring."

"Well, sit down. You shall have to eat it as it is."

Nancy carefully cut up the herring, and placed it before her husband. "How does it taste?"

"Marvellous," Benjamin said. "I have never tasted a fish like it."

There was a knock on the door. And who do you think it was? It was the Fishfinder. "Is that the herring?" he said, pointing to the fish. It had turned a strange colour.

"Yes," said Nancy. "My husband hung the herring up to keep it safe from the cat. But while he was out the cat knocked the logs from the hearth, and set his chair on fire. By the time I got back the herring was like this."

"What a disaster," said the Fishfinder. "Look at my poor herring now." Tears fell from his eyes, and dripped off his glasses.

"But it is the most marvellous fish I have ever tasted," said Benjamin. "I will always eat it smoked. Everyone should eat it smoked. Try some."

The Fishfinder tried some. Then smiled. "Since you found this wonderful way of eating herring I think it deserves a new name. As you were too tired to watch the fish properly, and the cat caused such a slip up, I shall name it a kipper."

Nancy and Benjamin thought it was a good name. The Fishfinder was happy.

So in the end, everything was all right. Benjamin liked the kipper very much and did not starve. The Fishmaker learned from his mistake, and no longer tells anyone what new fish he is making. And the Fishfinder spends all his time looking for new fish, instead of bothering the Fishmaker about making new ones.

**Luke Heeley** grew up in Stamford, Lincolnshire, and studied philosophy and literature at the University of Warwick. While there, he co-founded and co-edited *The Moebius*, a magazine of creative writing. He has performed at the Poetry Café in London and has poems in Issue 6 of *The Red Wheelbarrow*. This year, he won an Eric Gregory Award.

LUKE HEELEY

# Cleaning

The radio floods my ear
with sweet nothings. I fall asleep

in front of *Where Water Comes Together
With Other Water*. Through

the kitchen window I observe
my snoring double. A dog barks

somewhere. Sunlight snares
a galaxy of dust motes in its tractor beam

and I am back on the case,
unravelling cable as if I were a fireman

ready to do battle with an inferno. The vacuum
scratches over the threadbare rug.

I wipe down the piano. Underneath the lid,
the ivories are laughing to themselves.

# Reunion

A black dog slumbered by the fire,
its eyes flickering on the edge of oblivion.
I burnt some time
pumping coins into a fruit machine.
Its guts clanked as it puked back the metal.
"Ho there," croaked a familiar voice.
It was the Squire. We shook hands
and clasped each other in a stiff embrace.
He showed me the scars
from his recent hip-op before the talk
turned to Ben and his decline
into a life of octogenarian debauchery.
Understandable perhaps that he should
take up with a trophy wife, light Montecristos
from the stub of the last, snort
cocaine until he was blue in the face
after all those years alone in a cave.
The tabloids had had a field day. Our gossip
slipped down as easily as the bitter.
We skated over the topic of Hands.
Above us, a stuffed ferret froze,
forever in its preposterous leap.
A silence crept into our mouths
as the parents and screaming children
drove away in hatchbacks and space wagons.
Evening closed in and the Benbow emptied
until only we two remained.
The landlord called last orders at the bar.
We heard a banging at the door.
Blood pounded in my ears
as the Squire went to look outside
but there was no sign of Long John.

# The Splinter

MATT LEVINE was taking a bath. It had been a long time, longer than he could remember, since he'd last enjoyed a good soak. The water was very hot and his skin had turned scarlet. Sweat exuded from every pore. Steam clung to his thick-rimmed Buddy Holly glasses lying next to the basin. Realising that he couldn't tolerate the heat for much longer, he slipped down and dipped his head under the surface so that the water slowly swallowed up his face. Only his nose was not submerged now. A whooshing noise filled his ears, coming and going like waves. All his thoughts dissolved.

A thud from somewhere beyond the bathroom resonated in the tub.

That must be Sophie, he thought, rising up out of the water to listen. Her keys jangled as she put them down on the breakfast bar. He pictured her with the violin case under her arm as she lit a cigarette. She let out a long sigh.

He washed quickly then wrapped himself in a pistachio-coloured bathrobe. He liked pistachio.

Sophie was looking in the fridge for something to eat. Matt bent down to kiss her on the neck. She took out some cold cuts of chicken from the night before and offered him a wing.

"I've eaten already," he said. "How was your day?" The question came automatically.

"Don't ask. We were doing Bartok." She chewed on a piece of chicken skin. "You look like a lobster."

Their cat trotted into the kitchen on the prowl for a share of the meat.

"Haven't you fed him?" she said.

Matt shrugged. He had a special bond with the cat, whose name was Kaspar. He came from a litter of four kittens. Kaspar's eccentricity appealed to Matt. Often the cat would skid around the flat, chasing after non-existent mice. Matt had named him after the eponymous hero of Werner Herzog's film *The Enigma of Kaspar Hauser*, the tale of a mysterious boy found in a German market square in the nineteenth century. Sometimes, when Sophie was out, Matt would sit with Kaspar on the sofa, watching the television and wondering what was going on in the cat's mind. He was no closer to an answer now than ever before. Kaspar was indeed a mystery.

Werner Herzog was Matt's hero and the reason why he had wanted to become a film director in the first place. He was fifteen when, flicking through the channels in the early hours of the morning and supposedly asleep, he chanced upon *Aguirre: The Wrath of God*. From then on, he had only one object in his mind: to make films. Matt's first feature had come out six months ago to mostly lukewarm reviews. This didn't surprise him. *Flashpoint* was a crime caper and the last thing that British cinema needed. Matt didn't want to make genre movies for the rest of his life. He assumed that he would have to serve his dues before he could make the films he really wanted to make. The subject matter for his masterpiece, nevertheless, had eluded him.

"Some wine?"

He sauntered over to the overhead cupboard where they kept the wine glasses. As he pulled it open, the door flipped off its hinges and crashed to the floor, missing his bare feet by millimetres.

"Damn and fuck," he said, leaping out of the way. As he examined the damage, running his hand around the broken hinge, he felt a sharp pain at the end of his left index finger. Instinctively, he put the finger in his mouth.

"Are you OK?" Sophie said. "What happened?"

He pulled out the finger, glistening with spittle. Something thin and dark had found its way under the nail. "A splinter. I hate those bloody cupboards."

"Let me have a look." Sophie escorted him by the finger into the living room and inspected it under the lightbulb. "It's lodged deep. I don't think tweezers are going to get it out."

They both puzzled over the thin piece of wood.

"So what do I do then?" Matt said.

"Wait and see. The light's not good enough to get a proper look."

Sophie returned to the kitchen and brought back the large glasses of white wine.

They sat on the sofa and drank for five minutes. Sophie looked tired, Matt thought. Perhaps he should try and talk to her; but the splinter had made him withdraw into himself. He hated this splinter. Why should this have happened to him?

"Matty darling," Sophie said, laying her head on his shoulder, "I'm sleepy."

"Go to bed then." London seemed to do this to everyone, Matt thought. There wasn't a single person that you met who wasn't suffering from sleep deprivation. The whole city was constantly on the verge of a deep and ravenous slumber.

She placed her glass on the coffee table and wandered off to the bedroom. He heard her changing and then the buzzing of her electric toothbrush.

Matt switched on the television. The cricket highlights were just beginning. After the usual solid opening, England's middle order had been skittled out and was now facing an innings defeat at the hands of a rejuvenated Sri Lanka. He poured himself another large glass. The alcohol dulled the pain in his finger. Soon his body felt as if it were encased in rubber.

He opened the window and lit a roll-up that he had been saving. The view from the living room started with Muswell Hill and then stretched over the rest of London. At night, you could see all the way to the light on the Thames, the illuminated top of the Eye and part of the Millennium Dome. He liked the panorama. But the flat was beginning to bug him. That cupboard door falling off confirmed his instincts. It was time to get out of Muswell Hill. Time to move westwards to Hampstead or Belsize Park. Or maybe east to Angel or Hoxton. In his mind's eye, he pictured the new place – the floorboards would be made of Norwegian Yew. Was there such a thing as Norwegian Yew? That didn't matter. It sounded cool. The walls would be a pistachio green and the cupboards would be reinforced steel capable of withstanding an earthquake.

Still, he thought, as the cigarette smoke curled into the night, you had to admit that it was a fantastic view.


Matt sat at the desk in his tiny office off Tottenham Court Road flicking through a pile of scripts. The splinter had woken him up with a jolt at dawn and refused to let him go back to sleep. He had drunk six cups of Guatemalan Elephant coffee to pump him up but, now that noon was approaching, his caffeine fix had subsided and he was on the way down. His eyes felt heavy and sore as if he'd gone ten rounds with a seasoned heavyweight slugger.

The scripts he'd read through that morning were all variations upon a theme: crime capers, gangster movies, buddy flicks. They were called *The Sixth Paradigm*, *Personal Refusal*, *The Dirty and the Dead* and *Sawn-Off*. He never wanted to see another gangster, hood, conman or geezer. How he longed for real human drama: Herzog's ecstatic truth!

Beneath his fingernail, the splinter reminded him of its presence. He unbent a paperclip and began probing around under the nail, hoping to find some way of dislodging the intruding article. With an effort, he pushed the paperclip further in. An agonising bolt of pain struck. As soon as the paperclip had made contact with the splinter, it felt like a white-hot needle had been jabbed into his finger. He smarted and stifled a sob.

There was a dog-eared packet of Nurofen in the top desk drawer. Only one tablet remained. He swallowed it down without liquid, desperate for relief. The air-conditioning system whirred at a constant pitch, blocking the noise from outside. He had to get out of there. He wanted to lie down and sleep.

Fiona, his assistant, was standing by the coffee machine, waiting for a macchiato.

"I'm going early," he said to her.

"You look terrible, Matty," she said. "Are you alright?"

"No, I'm not so good. Take a look at this." He held his wounded finger aloft.

"What am I looking for?"

"Under the nail."

Fiona squinted and a look of displeasure dawned on her face. "Ooh. Nasty."

"You got any ideas on how to, you know, get it out of there?"

"Let's have a closer look."

She held the offending digit up to the light and studied it thoroughly.

"It's stuck right in there, isn't it?"

He grunted.

"Well, I can't see how you'll get at it with tweezers, short of taking the nail off altogether. No. Beats me."

With a series of gurgles and clicks, the coffee machine finished making the macchiato. Fiona released his hand and sauntered back to her desk. He headed for the lift.

"Matty," Fiona called after him. He turned around. Perhaps she had come up with something.

"Better keep an eye on it," she said. "In case it goes septic."

He squeezed out a thin smile. "Septic?"

"If your finger turns a funny colour then you should start to worry."

Once through the front door, he looked around with heavy eyes. The flat seemed strange to him in this afternoon light, as if the place had been taken by surprise and needed time to accommodate him.

He flung his leather jacket on the breakfast bar and slumped on to the sofa.

Alone with himself and the deathly quiet, he thought about Sophie. He imagined what she would be doing. Rehearsals had probably resumed. They would have just arrived back from lunch, He wondered where she had gone. Did she go alone or with someone else? It occurred to him that they rarely spoke about these things, the minutiae of day-to-day life.

His thoughts began to pool into one another, losing their distinctiveness; then, as if he were falling into a fathomless well, he sank into sleep.

He dreamed that he was in a boardroom, sitting opposite three women dressed in dark grey suits. The woman in the middle was doing the talking while the other two sat silently, their hands laid out on the table. She was interviewing him although he had no idea what it was for. His mouth moved in response. The words themselves eluded his grasp, popping like soap bubbles as soon as he tried to hold on to their meaning. Then the interviewer stood up and offered her left hand. He stood up and offered his. Her blank expresion turned to one of horror: a hideous, contorted mask of disgust. Looking down, his hand had become black, shrivelled and rotten. The women backed away. An insistent and mechanical vibration began to shake the boardroom.

Huge eyes stared at him and a wet sensation passed over his nose. Kaspar was purring loudly and licking his face.

He looked at the splinter once again. It hadn't budged. It was still fixed in there, under the nail of his left index finger. He could feel his heart racing and sweat breaking out on his forehead. This is enough, he thought. It's time to do something. He punched the number of his local surgery into the phone.

"St Mary's," a woman said.

"Hi. Can I get an appointment to see a doctor?"

"Who are you registered with?"

"I don't remember. It's not important. I just need to see someone. As soon as possible."

"Is it an emergency?"

"How do you mean, an emergency?"

"Is it a matter of life and death?"

He thought about his finger going septic, rotting and then falling off altogether. "Yes, it could well be. It's urgent."

Tip-tapping of fingers on a keyboard drifted up through the handset. "OK. We can fit you in the very last thing this evening. Six-fifteen. Your name?"

In the waiting room, a disappointed-looking man in a tweed suit was flicking through an old copy of *Country Life*. Jigsaws and stickle-bricks lay scattered on the carpet. There was no one else around, however, just Matt and the man in the tweeds. A pile of tattered magazines sagged next to a dingy fish tank. Matt flicked through a copy of *Reader's Digest* then wandered around. In a corner of the alcove, a plastic anatomical model of a human torso faced out towards the corridor. The model was designed for medical students and for biology classrooms. Matt remembered one just like it from school. He bent down and fiddled with the model. The left arm came away in his hand.

"Shit," he muttered, turning to see if anyone had seen him.

The man in tweeds looked over and grimaced when he saw what had happened. Matt tried to re-attach the arm back on but it refused to co-operate. Voices moved up and down the corridor. The surgery was quiet at this late hour. Matt hated coming to the surgery. Beneath his fingernail, the splinter pulsed, sending out shock waves of pain.

"Mr Levine?"

It was his turn. He placed the arm next to the model. The doctor stood half outside the consulting room.

She held the door open. Inside, he quickly took in the doctor's equipment: weighing scales, pale-green screen, stethoscope, couch, desk, out-of-date computer, blood pressure gauge and dozens of boxes containing samples from pharmaceutical companies.

He sat down. Three young people in white coats were lined up against the wall on the left. They gazed at him impassively.

"These are medical students," the doctor said. "They're here to observe the examination, Mr Levine. Do you have any objections?"

"Sure, why not?"

The badge on her shirt read Dr Rodchenko. He studied her features. She was tall and thin, in her late twenties, with short dark hair. She reminded him a little of Anouk Aimée in Federico Fellini's 8½. I wonder if she's been in the movies? he thought. She has good bone structure. A good look. The camera would love her.

"OK," she said. "So what can I do for you?"

"Well," he said, holding out his left hand. "It's this splinter, you see."

"Let's have a look at it in the light."

The three students leaned in, peering for a better view.

She tilted the hand one way and then the other. The doctor's hands were smooth and manicured. "Nasty. How long ago did this happen?"

"Yesterday evening."

She scribbled something down on a green pad. "Any symptoms of anything?"

"Just pain. A stabbing, throbbing pain."

"And you've had your tetanus jab, I see from your records."

The doctor leaned back and formed a steeple with her hands. She meditated on the issue of the splinter for what seemed to him like an eternity.

"Mr Levine, I'm afraid there's not too much that I can do for you in this case."

"Nothing? Surely you must be able to do something?"

"You can take Paracetomol if the pain gets too much ... Short of operating, I don't know how we can remove the offending article."

"But you mean it's just going to sit there? For ever? It's agonising."

The three students looked on as stony-faced as the Fates.

"In time, the splinter will emerge of its own accord."

"How so?"

"The body is truly an amazing thing, Mr Levine. When it senses that something foreign has invaded, it takes action. A remarkable contraption, all in all, I must say. Give it a couple of weeks and the splinter will be no more."

Matt lit the last of his pre-rolled cigarettes and paused by the newsstand next to the surgery's car park. He picked up a copy of the *Ham and High* and perused the 'Flats To Let' section. Rents had rocketed in the previous six months. With a red marker, he circled a potential place in Dartmouth Park. In his head, he made some quick calculations. If he took on *The Sixth Paradigm* and persuaded a big name actor to come on board then maybe they could stretch to somewhere better, he mused, before sliding into the car and setting off along the steep inclines around Muswell Hill. The traffic had thinned out and his passage home was smooth and unimpeded.

Sophie was cooking spaghetti carbonara when he arrived.

The cupboard door leaned against the breakfast bar.

"I'll fix that one of these days," Matt said, realising at the same moment that he had no idea whatsoever of how to mend it. He told her about the doctor.

"What did she have to say?" Sophie said.

"Nothing much. You know what they're like. It'll sort itself out."

They finished off the bottle of white wine and sat together on the sofa. Matt wrapped his arm around Sophie's shoulder.

"How was rehearsal?" he said. "Was Bartok any better today?"

Her eyes had closed. She murmured something incomprehensible in response. The light was fading, turning an odd shade of blue again. Neither of them had the energy to cross the room and switch on the light. Darkness had begun to leak into the corners of the flat but outside a few wisps of smoke reached up towards their twin in the sky. Further on, the Eye revolved, each pod reflecting the dusk. An occasional ripple moved outwards from his finger.

**Barbara Ferguson** was born in Ontario, Canada but has spent much of her life elsewhere, including Quebec, New Brunswick, Australia and Germany. *The Legend of the Vendors* is from *Line*, her novel in progress. Her work also appears in *Quo Vadis? An Anthology of Student Travel Writing* (J&R Reid Publishers, 2002). She hopes someone in Canada will pay her to be brilliant, but if that doesn't work she'll pick up and move on. Again.

## BARBARA FERGUSON

# The Legend of the Vendors
## FROM 'LINE'

*PEOPLE COME from all over the world to Line. They queue across the lawns for days, meeting neighbours, forging friendships, and eventually they reach the courtyard to consult the Eye. Each evening the vendors come along the Line with their wagons of goods to sell. This evening, one group of neighbours has gathered to share food and stories. The old man Khea is travelling alone, as is Grith, a young woman. Piri and her son Piribi have joined them, their blankets forming a brightly-coloured space for them all on the grass. As the day draws to a close, the news travels down the Line that the vendors are on their way.*

Piribi stood and craned his neck to see further up the Line, squinting into the dusk. "I think I see them! They've got big wagons!"

"That's them," Khea said. "They'll have to light their torches soon. Or maybe there's a while of light yet. We'll see."

"We're too far back! Let's go up there. Can we, Mama?"

A chorus of reproving adult voices answered him. "No jumping the Line!"

The boy's face fell. "I'll be sleepin' by the time they get here."

"There's lots of time, little one," his mother said, gathering him to her and settling him on her lap.

"They should've come sooner."

Khea raised a wagging finger. "Oh, no, young man, that they could not do. The vendors appear with the first shadows of the evening."

"Why?"

"For a very good reason," Khea said.

"It's traditional?" Wry humour curved Piri's mouth.

Khea nodded once. "That," he agreed, "and the shadows are essential to the story. You see, Piribi, vendors have been here as long as the Line has. A little longer, in fact. The first vendors appeared when only the people who lived here knew that the Eye even existed. This was so long ago that it was during the times when the people and the animals still spoke the same language."

"Animals can't talk!"

"Can't they? They talk to each other. They probably talk to the trees and the wind, and the water in the woods. But we don't understand their language any more, partly because of what happened here all those centuries ago. I suppose I'd better tell you.

"Now, you have to imagine that these lawns were not so wide here. Those trees there were much taller, almost touching the sky, and they stood much closer together, like the fingers on your hands. And there were many more trees then. There were so many that this place was not a lawn at all, but a forest. There were shady glens and trails that the animals and people used for hunting food or gathering plants. It wasn't that unusual, in those days, to see a woman and a bear walking together, wondering about the fishing that day.

"For a while, after the people found the Eye, they would make their ways through the woods to ask it their Questions. There was no space to line one behind the other, so they used to wait in groups, little clusters between the trees, and whoever was closest to the Eye would go first, and so on. So the people would wait, and could lean against the trees, talking to each other or to the animals, who would come to keep them company. The animals enjoyed our conversation, you see, and I suppose we enjoyed theirs. It's always interesting to talk to someone new and different.

"Eventually the animals became very curious about the Eye, and asked the waiting people about it. 'It is an amazing find,' the people told the animals. 'This will answer life's biggest Question. What should you do? Where should you go? Should you marry? It will answer whatever we need to know.' The animals were very impressed, as you might imagine, and for a while they asked the people everything about their Questions, and what the Eye was like. And at night, when the waiting people were asleep under the trees, the woodland creatures would whisper together in their dens and nests.

"'I would ask where to find the best fish,' the father bear told his cubs.

"'I would ask how to avoid the owl,' shivered the mouse.

"'I would ask if it is time to leave the den,' one fox kit murmured to her brother.

"And so it went. Then one night, when the moon was full and the animals could meet, they gathered together in a secret glade and decided that they, too, wanted to ask the Eye.

'Tomorrow,' they promised, 'we will join the people between the trees, and we will ask the Eye our Questions.'

"So just after sunrise of the next day, an amazing assortment of animals flew, pranced, lumbered and wormed their way through the maze of trees and found the people just waking. 'We're here to see the Eye!' the animals said happily.

"'Oh, indeed?' the people said, not very pleasantly, I'm afraid. 'And just what would you ask our Eye?' Well, as the animals shared their various Questions, the people started to laugh. They laughed louder and louder and the sound echoed through the forest morning. The animals were dismayed, and demanded of the people, 'Why do you laugh?'

"'What utter nonsense!' the people said. 'We won't let you waste the Eye's time with such ridiculous Questions.' And they chased the animals away."

Piribi blinked in the reddened light of the afternoon. "Mama says no question is ridic'lus." Piri's arms tightened around him.

"She's right," Khea said. "But these people weren't as smart as you and your mother, I guess. You remember that this is very long ago. Things were different then.

"The animals met in the glen again that night. The first sliver of the moon was gone, but there was still enough light to see that everyone was very angry. 'How dare those people chase us away!' the animals said to one another. For the first time, the stag thought about how much damage his antlers could do to thin human skin. Raven sharpened his beak, with thoughts as dark as his feathers. Bear's claws scored the trees and earth in anger. The animals made so much noise with their growling and grumbling that the drowsy people heard it, and were a little afraid, because the sound was new and strange and full of bitterness.

"But in the glade, the muttering stopped when someone – some stories say it was the rabbit, some say the wolf, still others, the owl – proposed to take revenge on the laughing humans, saying, 'Their shuttered eyes don't see well in the shadows. If we came upon them by night they would hardly know what was happening.'

"Now I'm sorry to say that some creatures immediately suggested trampling the people to death, or otherwise hurting them. There are always those who wish to do grievous harm. But the animal who had spoken first disagreed. It said, 'If we had some of their clothing, and worked together to prepare, we could accomplish something similar to what they did to us. We could make them feel foolish and ridiculous.' The fiercer ones did not look entirely satisfied, so it added, 'Perhaps the people will turn on each other and do each other harm. Then we would not even soil hoof or claw with their blood.'

"This was much better received, and all the animals agreed immediately to work according to the plan. Climbers of all sorts took to the trees, swiftly and silently leaping through the branches, back to the people's sleeping grove. They crept down the tree trunks and along the mossy ground, and snatched cloaks, coverlets, tunics and breeches, bearing their cloth burdens back into the dark trees and away through the woods.

"In the meantime, the other animals began gathering the very juiciest berries and fruit, the ripest vegetables and sweetest honey, carrying it all back into the grove. Birds combed their nests for the most lustrous feathers, and persuaded Peacock to donate several from his tail. Even the magpies offered the best of the shiny baubles they'd collected. River rats and fish worked together to pull up the prettiest shells and most excellent pearls from the sandy depths.

"Along the riverbanks, otters patted earth into pot-like forms, as they had often watched humans do, and in the glade, birds nested twigs together, twigs larger than they had ever handled, into reedy baskets. Spiders helped, too, weaving their silk into strong slender straps to carry the baskets. As the sun began to lighten the forest, the animals piled their treasures into the containers. 'Let's go!' they shouted.

"But the animal who had started it all was much wiser. 'Now is not the time,' he – or possibly she – said. 'We have worked well together, but we have worked all night. Now we must sleep and be ready for another night's work. Remember, human eyes do not see so sharply as ours, once the sun sets. We will wait for the shadows to help us, and will be well rested besides.'

"The other animals saw the sense in this, and returned to their homes for a day's rest. If the people noticed the absence of animals that day, they probably didn't think much of it. After all, the people had their own Questions to ask the Eye, and if they were not waiting to ask, they were busy with their own households. But as the day stretched on, and the sun's light faded to the very colour it is now, the animals began to awaken."

Khea paused. He could hear new voices, confident and raucous, drifting back over the Line toward the little group. His audience, for their part, seemed not to be aware of any outside noise. They were listening in stillness, waiting for him to continue. He smiled a little and went on.

"They had planned this carefully. The clothes they had stolen had been gently slashed or nibbled along the seams, to fit over haunches and forepaws, and the cloaks were large enough to hide any very un-human tails. The creatures balanced on one another's shoulders while birds and squirrels helped dress them in human clothing. The baskets and earthenware containers of treasures were slung over shoulders or held tightly in paws, and then they were ready.

"Now the people, who were just thinking about their evening meal and settling themselves down to rest after a day's waiting, could scarcely believe their eyes when these shapes appeared out of the forest. They blinked and squinted, but the cloaks and shadows were just enough to hide the features of the newcomers. Then the people saw the flashing and glinting of the wares, and heard the calls of the strange new folk. 'Fresh fruit and treasures!' the costumed animals were calling, disguising their voices as best they could. 'We have the best honey! Berries ripe to bursting! The perfect pearl to offer your beloved!'

"Well, as you can imagine, the people forgot about the mystery of who these figures were, and began climbing over each other to see the baskets of goods. They exclaimed and squabbled, pushed one another out of the way, and clamoured to be the first to own these fantastic things. Now money had not really been thought of in these times, but everybody had something they thought they might trade for these new delights. Oh, they offered all kinds of things: woolen mittens, carved flutes, glittering stones – anything they could think of that might have value to these mysterious and sudden vendors.

"The animals were very amused and greatly enjoyed themselves, trying not to laugh as they kept the wares out of human reach, demanding more and higher prices for the trade. 'Two mittens and a flute, for this exquisite pearl? Surely not! Why, that woman there has offered a tunic and her own new sandals!' And so it went, until suddenly the animals realized the moon was high above and their baskets were empty. They tried to retreat back into the forest, but the people wouldn't let them go. They had to promise to return the next day with more to trade. Finally, they escaped to report to the others back in the glade. The humans lay themselves down to sleep curled around their new treasures. They heard the noise of animal laughter through the darkness and wondered what it was.

"The animals had a very busy time of it then. After some debate, they decided that the nocturnals should begin the task of gathering new treasures while the daylight creatures slept, then reverse the roles. Daylight made the task more challenging, as the animals had to slink and dart through the forest to avoid the humans, all the while searching out and carrying back the newest items for that night's sale.

"The people, however, had been discussing things in the meantime. They compared the prices they had paid and quickly concluded that they had been unfairly treated. True, the goods were special, they were lovely and bright, but many of the people had gotten so caught up in the bargaining that they had hardly known how much of their own property they had traded away. In the clear light of the day they realized it, and because they were angry with themselves they were furious with the vendors. 'This time,' the people said, 'we will be prepared.' They began to gather rocks and sharpen sticks, to attack the vendors if the prices got too high.

"But like the animals in the forest, there was a thoughtful member of the group who halted the people in their preparations. It was an old man, and he, like his woodland counterpart, pointed out the benefits of working together."

"Was he as old as you?" Piribi asked.

His mother looked chagrined, and Grith laughed.

Khea smiled. "Oh, maybe even older. My hair is gray, but this man's was silver, a bright, shining silver like moonbeams on the water, and his beard rippled from his chin to his knees.

"'Staying here as a group will undo us,' the old man said. 'If we had sentries in the woods, we could watch on all sides for their approach, and warn our neighbours with a whispered message, passed person by person across the grove. Then if any one of us sees the vendors coming, we would all soon know from which direction, and surround them before they realize what is happening.' This idea was met with much cheering and applause. Then someone else pointed out the benefits of removing low branches and scrub from the grove, so that their line of sight would be widened. After all, people find it difficult enough to see in the gathering dark, without mistaking every branch for a person. So they set about clearing their space of extra foliage and debris, and made it as open as they could. And just before dusk, they arranged themselves in a loose line in the shadows of the trees, looking outward through their clearing at the darkening forest beyond. Some few were left in the middle of the grove, so as to appear as eager for the sale as everyone had been the night before.

"Now the animals were so excited about their plan, and so weary from the day's exertions, that they approached in their disguises without much caution. Their keen eyes should have seen the sentries in the wood and should have noticed the much-diminished number of people in the grove. And if their excellent ears had been listening properly, they would have heard the excited whisper as it traveled down the line of waiting watchers.

"As they stepped into the clearing with their trays full of treasures, they noticed the old man, his silver hair gleaming in the fading light. 'Now!' he cried, and they were mystified only as long as it took for the people to leap out and attack. It was sudden and violent. As you might imagine, the balanced animals soon fell off one another and the people realized what they were actually fighting.

"At first the people did not know whether to keep striking or to laugh. The animals were blinking and floundering in the clearing, and the smaller ones struggled free and bounded into the woods to hide. Those who could not run as quickly, or who were injured, heard the old man call 'Enough!' Then he walked forward into the tangle of legs and hooves and whiskers and paws.

"The animals were suddenly very afraid. They tried to explain, but the old man interrupted.

"'I know what you wanted to do,' he said, and I think he was sad.

"'Return to the forests,' he commanded. 'The Eye is not for you. These treasures are not for us. Stay near your homes and keep to the deep woods. We can no longer live in harmony. We will live apart and teach our children to keep their distance from you and yours.' He flung the trays into the woods, and there was a sigh from the people watching, because they would've loved to have had more of those excellent fruits and gleaming jewels.

"The animals climbed to their feet and returned to the forests with slow reluctance. The people made no further move to strike, but watched them go, and both sides were wishing things had turned out differently. The animals returned to the grove, and passed on the message, and that night some of the people heard another strange new sound through the trees, that of the sighing and weeping of the animals. But there were some people who did not hear it, over the noise of their own sorrow.

"Since that day, the animals have lived in their places and we in ours. Slowly more people heard about the Eye, and traveled to ask it Questions. Slowly we cleared more of the forest around the Eye, so that we wouldn't be surprised again. We arranged ourselves so that messages could travel easily and we could mark anyone's approach. And slowly the language changed, in the wood and in our towns, so much so that one language became many, and we can no longer understand the animals, nor they understand us.

"And the vendors," Khea paused. "The vendors are people like us now. But still, they only arrive as the shadows do."

His audience realized that the noise that had been building steadily in the background was almost upon them. They turned as the heavy wheels of the first wagon trundled over the grass to their left, and their faces were lit with a sudden harsh light as the first of the torches was set ablaze.

**Helen Stephen** is 23 years old and originally from Newcastle-upon-Tyne. She has been studying in St Andrews since 1997, obtaining an Honours Degree in English and Medieval History before beginning the Creative Writing M.Litt. Helen has been interested in comic writing ever since she was refused permission to put on her satirical nativity play at school, for fear of offending the Christian Union. History continues to be a passion for Helen, particularly the spooky folklore surrounding the closes and wynds of St Andrews and Edinburgh. Among her ambitions is the desire to write the definitive ghost story. She funded her degree by working in a sweet shop.

## HELEN STEPHEN

# Sugar High

THERE WERE TEN MINUTES to go before my shift began. I was standing half dressed before an open freezer, trying to squeeze myself into my uniform and grab cartons of ice cream at the same time. I've contracted repetitive scoop injury from my job. Serving endless double chocolate chip cones to snivelling, impatient toddlers is beginning to subtract seriously from my maternal instinct.

I work part-time at Rose Mendrix Traditional Chocolate Emporium. This is not a choice. This is my do-or-die card, being played every day of my degree. I don't expect that any student job is a picnic. I once spent a December vacation sealing seven thousand envelopes so that I could pay for Christmas presents. But the Rose Mendrix experience is unlike anything I've ever encountered.

My manager, Carla, is a highly-strung chain smoker, and has a habit of leaving the shop for a cigarette whenever a large and demanding queue builds up. She has irritable bowel syndrome and hair the colour of burnt-sienna, courtesy of her husband, who owns a chain of beauty salons across Scotland. The I.B.S. is courtesy of the enormous, pungent lunches she brings to work – sausage, liver and potato salad being a memorable example. She always smells of strong cigarettes, and has one of those faces that have actually developed sunken wrinkles along the cheeks, giving her the appearance of perpetually taking a deep draw of nicotine. When she's there, the shop alternates between smelling of fags, her meaty lunches or her frequent trips to the toilet. I can never understand how people are tempted to buy chocolate in such a noisome environment.

But it's not all bad. On mornings like this, when it's misty and cool outside and the shop is quiet, I can often spend a few pleasant hours perched on the stool behind the till, reading and occasionally helping myself to a delicious Rose Mendrix caramel truffle, its perfect chocolate roundness just the right size to slip into my mouth when no one is looking.

Before I settled down with my book, I scanned Carla's red-penned list of things to do. The first task read COONT THE MONEY IN THE SAFE. Carla writes exactly as she speaks, and once iced HAPPY XMAS FAE SANTA on a chocolate reindeer. Intriguingly, someone bought it.

I scored out the first task. The only person who ever does safe-counts is Carla. My student colleagues, Sarah and Liza, share my profound conviction that, provided we don't arrive at work to discover the windows smashed and a large hole blasted in the safe door, the chances are that the float money stored therein will add up to exactly what it did the previous day. We'd operated on this assumption for months until Carla tried to catch us out by removing two hundred pounds and hiding it in the microwave. She successfully proved our negligence, but in the end it backfired on her when, after two days and a particularly stressful morning, she had a burning urge for tomato soup. I was serving a triple ice cream to a young boy out front when I heard the ping of the microwave, followed by a bestial, bloodcurdling howl from Carla. Not only did she have a lengthy and humiliating report to fax to head office, but the boy managed to sneak away in the ruckus without paying for his cone.

I had to ring Carla before I could relax into my book. This morning while unlocking the door, a dribble of rainwater splashed on my head and I glanced up at the shop sign. Some of the letters had been removed and it would be better to warn her before she saw it for herself. I dialled her mobile.

"Hello?"

I could hear a radio and a hairdryer going in the background.

"Hi Carla it's me."

"What? What have you done?"

"Oh, nothing, it's just the shop sign. Some of the letters are gone."

"Bloody students! I'm sick and tired of your lot doing this to my shop. Head office are going to want my blood for this. We'll leave it for a few days."

"I don't really think that we can."

"Why not?" The hairdryer stopped and I could imagine her waving at her husband and those around her to be silent. Carla hates being told what to do; she hates even being advised what to do.

"Well, like I said, some of the letters are missing. Not all. It reads…differently."

"What do you mean? What does it say?"

"It says…well, um…it still says Traditional Chocolate Emporium, but…"

"What does it say?"

"It says…it says semen…Traditional Chocolate Emporium."

"WHAT? How the hell?"

"Well, they took the R and the O, and then they took DRIX. So now it reads little s, little e, big M, e, n, Traditional Chocolate Emporium. Semen. Traditional Chocolate…"

"That is disgusting. Fucking disgusting."

"It's actually quite clever when you think about it. I mean, disgusting. But quite ingenious."

"Get on to head office. I'll be in after my hair's dry." The line went dead.

I decided I'd better get on with her list. STACK SHELVES. Going up and down the cold-room ladder to retrieve boxes of sugary produce is made difficult by the Rose Mendrix uniform. It consists of a shapeless viscose blouse of the sort favoured by obese, adulterous women on American talk shows. This is teamed with a mud-brown wrap-around skirt of an unfortunate mid-calf length. Together with flat shoes, it adds ten pounds to Carla, Sarah and myself. Poor Liza is already overweight and in her uniform she looks like a brandy truffle.

The problem is the skirt's tendency to flap dangerously wide open at the slightest movement. I once entertained a van-load of builders on their lunch break when I was attempting to dress the Easter window without being arrested for indecent exposure. They kept blaring their horn and yelling get 'em oot for the lads and my face grew steadily more puce every time I reached up to fasten giant cardboard eggs to the ceiling and revealed a couple more inches of thigh and God-knows what else to them.

The same thing happens when reaching to stack the high shelves, and it was thus I found myself teetering on a stool as I tried to balance a box of chocolate peanuts on one leg without fully exposing the other. I had just started to fill the top shelf when the door opened, blasting the shop with cold morning breeze.

"Eh…pet?"

I twisted around and looked down at a small, red-faced man clutching a white plastic bag. I recognised him. He often came in to buy dark chocolate brazils for his wife – or so he always said – but today he looked unusually excitable.

"Have ye got scales in here, pet?" he asked, breathlessly. He was beginning to turn purple.

I stepped down from the stool, trying not to model my underwear to the man. He was quite flustered enough already.

"Yes – for weighing the chocolates…" I tailed off as he thrust the plastic bag in my face. I caught a strong and not entirely fresh waft of smoked haddock.

"Can ye weigh my fish for me, pet?" He waved the bag at me again.

"Your fish?" The customer is always right.

"Aye. Haddock. For the wife," he elaborated with a wink. I swallowed hard and took the bag between two rigid fingers.

"Just a moment, sir." I glanced at the shiny stainless steel surface of the scales and gulped at the prospect of some aggrieved customer returning haddock-scented pralines to Carla. I looked back at the man. He was beaming encouragingly, and my heart went out to him in all his florid glory. My heart rarely goes out to customers, so I put the slimy bag onto the steel plate and waited for the digital light to come on.

"That's...nine hundred and three grams, sir," I said, hastily removing the bag and offering it to him.

"Can ye tell me what that is in poonds?"

"I'm sorry, sir, I haven't a clue."

"Have ye no conversion chart?"

"I'm sorry sir, we only work in grams." It's only 2002.

"You're the opposite of me then. Ach well, thanks anyway, pet." He stuffed the bag into his coat pocket. I grimaced.

"No problem, sir."

"You never can tell when they're trying to cheat you," he said, esoterically, and with that was gone, passing Carla as she rushed in from the salon. Her hair was a vibrant orange and had been dried into a sort of ducktail. She stank of cigarettes.

"What did Mr McLellan want? Brazils, was it?" She hung up her coat and sprayed breath freshener liberally down her throat.

"He wanted me to weigh his fish..." I said, uncertain whether this violated company health and safety policy.

"Och, aye," she replied. OK, so that was normal.

"Except I couldn't tell him what it was in pounds."

"Don't they teach you anything in Yoo-nee-versity these days, then?" Carla tutted.

"I've got an English degree."

"Aye, but you'd think that for what ye pay they'd throw in some simple sums. Now am I wrong?"

After lunch, Carla stood outside, musing over the desecrated sign with a mournful expression and smoking. The ice cream window was open in front of her and whenever she exhaled, a cloud of acrid smoke billowed over the sugar cornets. I silently filled up silver trays of chocolates, cursing this woman who reminded me regularly to wash my hands because you never know where students have been but had no qualms about blowing smoke over fresh ice cream.

An eccentrically made-up old woman toddled into the shop wheeling a bulging shopping bag behind her. She paused in front of the till, removing her gloves and mumbling. I watched her as I stacked cappuccino truffles in a pyramid. Finally she put down her bag and fixed me with a baleful blue eye.

"I'd like some toffee, please," she said.

I hate this perhaps more than anything. She had walked past an enormous plastic bin filled to the hilt with bags of toffee of every conceivable size and flavour in order to reach her post in front of the till. I am not paid enough to do people's shopping for them, particularly not old ladies with hairy faces whose teeth are stained with globs of pink lipstick.

"What flavour would you like, ma'am?"

"Flavour? I don't know. Just toffee flavour."

I ground my teeth. "We have about fifteen different flavours. Would you like to come with me so I can show you?"

"I'm not going anywhere. I've a bad hip. Just get me some toffee, there's a good girl."

"Shall I choose a flavour for you?"

"No! I don't like all these fancy flavours. Just get me plain."

"We don't actually have plain flavour. We have vanilla, though."

"Aye, vanilla. That's what I said."

I retrieved a small bag of vanilla toffee and rang it up on the till. "That's ninety-five pence, please," I said, putting it in a small bag and offering it to her.

"It is diabetic, isn't it?"

Of course it isn't fucking diabetic. Think back – did you ask me for diabetic, you old goat? Now we have to go through the flavour rigmarole again. I noticed a stray hazelnut truffle by my foot and squashed it, very slowly and deliberately, into the floor, smiling politely – that's the Rose Mendrix way – all the while.

As I was finally bagging up her diabetic toffee, the woman was kind enough to point out a rogue orange mousse chocolate that had rolled under the till and out onto the floor by her feet, where it lay, dusty and burst open, weeping bright orange slime.

"You should wipe things like that up, a person could slip and kill themselves," she chastised, helpfully.

I considered inviting her to demonstrate her theory but instead handed her the toffee and went through the back to get a damp cloth. She was still standing there when I came back, clearly determined to supervise the removal of the hazardous mousse. The same thing happens when grinning, demonic children slop their ice creams all over the floor. The mothers' eyes flash angrily at me, as if it's my fault that their offspring are so badly co-ordinated. All I can do is gnash my teeth and lock my face into a meek and demure freeze-frame while I mop up the mess.

I spent the rest of the afternoon gift-wrapping, and the time passed quickly. Suddenly there were only ten minutes to go before my shift ended. A woman in a navy suit and heels entered the shop. She smiled at me as she approached the till and looked like she was in a hurry and knew what she wanted. Thank God. Finally, a nice, normal, sane customer who won't give me any hassle.

"I want to return a faulty bag of chocolates," she said, brusque and perfumey.

"Of course. What was the problem?" I asked, waiting while she delved in her bag for the offending product. She passed a crumpled bag over the counter. It had been opened and most of its contents devoured. "These are…factory rejects, madam. They aren't actually refundable as they were on sale anyway."

"Yes. They're all a funny shape."

I paused. "Well, they're rejects. We sell them cheap because they aren't perfect. They taste just as good but their shape or colour isn't quite…"

"All twisted, one of them was. My husband was quite upset."

"Well, unfortunately, as I say, they're not actually returnable."

"Cash will be fine, although I paid by card."

I met her eye for a long moment. She was wearing blue eyeliner, giving her a surprised expression, and her eye shadow had creased along the wrinkles of her eyelid. "I'm afraid I can't give you a cash refund if you paid by credit card," I began, firmly. "What about an exchange for another product? I'll give you a few minutes to choose something."

With that I turned around and began gift-wrapping a box of Belgian truffles, hoping I'd made it clear that the conversation was over without being rude enough to lose my job. I can deal with Carla, and cleaning the slimy ice cream freezer, but the most difficult thing about student jobs is having to endure being spoken to so rudely without any possibility of a comeback. I once had a woman attempt to pay for goods with a cheque that had been written six months ago, for a different amount, and made out to a different shop. When I refused the sale, she told me she hated me and would do everything in her power to have me fired. There's nothing you can do about these people.

I finally sold my customer a small bag of sugared almonds, and I closed the sale with one eye on the clock, not wanting to remain in the company of Carla and the sticky smell of chocolate for one minute beyond my designated shift. After a brief wrangle with the woman over five-pound notes – she wanted an English one, the till only had Scottish, and like many customers, she was reluctant to listen to my patient explanation that as long as it says pounds sterling it is legal British tender – I was finally free to go.

It could be worse, I told myself, as I went to change. I have friends who clean pub toilets on a Sunday morning. And this must all be part of what my mother calls life's rich tapestry whenever I complain. I stuffed my precious payslip into my bag and shut my locker. I was heading to the library to start an essay, which put me in mind of brain-food.

Would one more caramel truffle be missed? I doubted it. After the string of eclectic customers, I damn well deserved it. I popped one in my mouth on my way out the door, biting down and savouring the thick ooze of caramel over my teeth: heaven. If it weren't for Carla and the customers, I sometimes think I could work here for free.

**Heather Murray** spent her whole life in south-east Michigan before studying abroad in St. Andrews at the tender age of 21. Having seen some of the world she graduated with a BA in English Literature from the University of Michigan in Ann Arbor. To facilitate her studies she has worked these past four years in various positions in academic libraries. In the future she intends to obtain a Masters in Library Science.

## HEATHER MURRAY

# Grandmother

Once I had an ideal picture
that she would smell of lilac and liniment,
and she would cradle me
with a hand-knit afghan over her knees
and share the stories of her life
through photographs yellowed by age.

But her hugs are swift and bony.
There was no comfortable chair
nor wistful remembrances for her.
She stands at her kitchen counter
above pocked brown skin
blotched like her own hands.
My grandmother,
peeling potatoes.

# Another Rapunzel

But now I have taken my hair
into my own hands.

With kitchen scissors
blunted by misuse
I have railed against
the witch's wishes
and given myself permission.

Snip.
The scissors are my friendly weapon.
Click.
Here they skim the nape.
Whisper.
Air moves, filling empty space.

My fingers sift these
weightless tendrils,
leave them scattered
loosely at my feet,
a token.

As a butterfly
breaks free
I release myself,
exiled from this hirsute tower.

# Jack

He escaped monotony of cow and mother
by scaling up a bean stalk,
but swung back down after meeting
an ogre and his wife,
after trying to eat him.
Jack Tartare on the lunch menu.

For riches plucking at his wildest imaginings—
a singing harp, the hen that laid golden eggs.
For his Twenty-four Carat Breakfast
he returned up the stalk
braving that carnivorous lair.
Jack's life-wish.
This poor man's opportunity.

# Making the Bed

In my room the duvet
is out of place
and the pillow makes
a lumpy landscape
on the mattress canvas.

In the early morning
when he is gone
and I have nearly dressed
I tuck the sheets in tight,
shake the duvet straight
and smooth down the cotton cover.
Then I can place the pillows side-by-side.

# Phoning Grandfather

I hear the weakened voice,
scratchy from sickness
and too many hospital tests.
Our sixty seconds of conversation—
I say,
*I love you, I miss you,*
*and as much as possible,*
*I hope you are doing well.*
He says,
*I love you too, but*
*you should not have left home.*
I try not to cry.
He continues,
*I am still proud of you.*
*I still love you, but*
*I think you were mistaken.*
Our last ever conversation
thousands of miles apart.

**Dawn Baumgarten** is from Chicago, Illinois. She is interested in creative writing, slam poetry, linguistics and philosophy.

DAWN BAUMGARTEN

# Operator

I USUALLY GET FED after the high-heeled ladies leave. But Mother's heels clomping on the kitchen tiles, and cupboards slamming, were telling me that my tummy's grumbling wasn't gonna go and shut up any time soon. And worse than the *clompity-clomp* and the *creakity-slam* and the *gurr-growl* was Mother's face crinkled up like one of those papier-mâché dolls I made at school. Mother was saying that we had to have ourselves a little chat before I could go on and help myself to the leftovers from the party. Her fingernails were tapping on the white counter-top to the words she pointed a finger to. But her words didn't seem to be going the way her finger pointed, 'cos her voice came out hard through a pout that made the words swerve down and away from me. I liked the sound of her nails. But I didn't like the way her voice didn't go good with the nice tapping sound.

She pointed and tapped and said, "Your behavior was inexcusable tonight, do you hear me? Inexcusable!" I wondered if it had something to do with me sneezing from the blue-high-heeled lady's cigarette smoke. I was going to say so but she didn't give me a chance. She tapped and pointed and said, "You can't talk out loud to the heater when my friends are near. Didn't you hear Dr. Fletcher tell you to speak clearly to other people not to yourself or to, well, to a *heater*?" I asked her why. But that question just got her to take away the food she was stretching out to set down before me. I heard the dish break in the sink but don't remember the sound of her pulling up a chair beside me.

I heard her say something about having it 'up to here' with me questioning her all the time. I looked for her fingertip to draw the line where 'up to here' hit. But her pointer finger just went tapping right along with the other ones. She went on talking and shaking her head and she even added a stomping of one shoe, saying all the while, "You promised me and Dr. Fletcher to speak *clearly* and to ask *normal* questions." I was near about ready to go ahead and ask what were 'normal' questions, but I got to thinking maybe that wouldn't be a 'normal' question to start off with. But she kept asking me if I was hearing her, like I went and lost my ears or something, saying, "Don't you hear me? People don't get you!" I didn't say nothing after that, 'cos it wouldn't be like me to want people to get me. Doesn't she know that with most games it's all about trying to get away from being got?

So I got as far away from her as I could. I got as far from her as upstairs and into the bathroom so I couldn't hear her voice snap shut with the slamming of the door.

I'm getting even nearer, nudging up close to my heater. Here by the heater, I am clear of her words. All I can hear is the *heave-ho* of Stuffy's breath through the vents of the heater. Stuffy lives through those vents. Way down in the basement his heart hides in the fire of the furnace. Stuff's breath isn't fire. But he breathes through the heater with enough heated breaths to warm me. So I like to get as near as I can to the heater, as near as I need to take all I can from what comes from the heat. I get naked in the bathroom. Up here, pressed up against the vents, I get nude. I get as bare as I need to get so as to get all I can from the heat. I got to get down to stripped even though Mother says not to. But she's not down there tonight. Nor can she see down to where my hand goes, down to where there's a dip in the upper slit of my curved hips. Mother said she carried me between her hips once for months and months.

But Mother isn't near where I am, not near enough to whisper – what not to do or what to do or that my doing so is bad. No, tonight is not like last night when Mother made me wear patent leather shoes with bows. She's not pointing where to pass a silver tray to the ladies playing Bridge. She's not pressing me into a corner with a pinch to the ear saying, "Mind your manners, young lady." Even if he's bigger by far, she should mind my smelly brother more than me. She should mind what Toddo did to the floor before the tip-toe trot of the high-heel ladies came. Toddo made the white gleam of *my* polish on *her* floor scuffed up yuck with puke. Can't Mother see it's Todd who doesn't know how to play fair? And here's a clearly *normal* question for her to be asking herself: How can Toddo prepare for the play of house when he's always playing rough house with himself and not cleaning up after?

Mother should go on and mind her own mind. She scolds me for feeding leftovers to the garbage disposer. I mind her calling him such an awful name as that. I yell at her to call the garbage disposer "Stuffy." Well, "Stuff" is his proper name. She says, "Mind your tone with me, missy." She should hear how silly she sounds answering a 'why' with a 'because I said so.'

I mind her ways of making me take a bath. She tells me to take turns. Well she should take a turn and listen to me. But no, she just bends over to whisper a 'time and out' to me, cups her mouth to tell a hushed 'this and that' to some lady. I only tell her not to do the whispers to other people when I am near. I mind secrets. I am mindful of tattle-talers and tall tales, short ends of tales told – some *sh-thing* about me maybe going back to the place where there was the pretty lady all in white. Did I disturb her peace and quiet time, telling her what the nice lady told me about me being there 'cos of me being special and all? Or did I say some *sh-thing* to her friends about Toddo doing something to the tiles when she was away? I'm not just talking about him up-chucking 'till it looked like there was a big ol' food fight right in our very own kitchen. No, after what he did this time, the tiles could not erase back to white, not with all the Spic 'n' Span in the bucket. The tiles took a turn from white to a red that I wouldn't even call red. It's the same red that blurs up from under the black tracks down his arms. I didn't yank her head down to Stuff's grated lips to hear his growls gossip or to listen to words so heated that they melt to a *hiss*.

If it weren't for what Mother calls the disposer or what I call Stuffy, the connector, the long-term terminator, the heater, and the grinder-upper – you know, the gimongous thing that eats the leftovers, the humammoth thing that the print around the steel rim of the drain says 'In-Sink-Erator.' Well, I can't even get a say on what would've happened by now if I hadn't had some help from certain household conveniences. Do tell, did you feed the garbage disposal when you were a little one? Did they call the grinder-upper-ma-gig an 'In-Sink-Erator' in your house? Just between you and me, those names are the same as the names the girls called me closed in a ring-around-the-rosey. Those names are all rather bound up like hunger – sounds rub so close together, it seems to me, real sneak-like, tile-to-tile tight so that the cracks don't show.

There would be no need for 'out of bounds' with them there names: Food Grinder, Air Conditioner, Central Heating. With Stuff's whys and whens, who ever knows how he works? How does anyone know where the water he guzzles goes, the food he munches stays, the heat he breathes comes from? Not 'when' or 'how', but 'why' is what I want to know. Why would Mother say to Father, "Our boy is messed up. Denial, denial, you're in denial, Doug"? Why would Dad say to Mom, "OK, OK, let's not lie, Lynn"?

Why not say so in front of me—the girl who saw a crack in the tile turn red from a needle's slip through tracks on the back of her brother's arm? Me, the sister who heard her brother and not in a whisper, say, "Ah my little friend, my girl elfling, my very own fairy, what do you want on your sandwich? Lettuce, bacon, onion, tomato? Let's play our word game. Come on little one, let me change the word 'lettuce' to *let us*, let yourself hear the word 'bacon' as *become*, let us make the word 'onion' into *union* and turn 'tomato' into yours truly: *Toddo!* Come, come here: Let us – become – union – with Toddo!"

Tomato spat red like the hole in his skin; his cut splat drops of blood to *smack*, became hide-and-seek in cracks of tile, a run and run-on and spin-quick like you'll never see the end of all those spun-out veins, wrung thin, tied down, undone. I am done playing. "In the corner with you and no peek-a-boo," was what the girl – who saw what she should not have seen, heard from the boy – who should not have been doing what he had done to himself.

Their sounds: children playing, or other mothers playing cards, half of a conversation spoken in whispers, are sounds that don't need me to be made. Their sounds are all around me but too quiet for me to get a good hear of. In their noise, in the cover of voices, which should be a comfort, in the crowd of them, nothin' near better than what here contains.

I ran naked from the bath as fast as I could to get here – here next to the heater, where I am turning my fingers to braid my hair as it dries in Stuff's breath. But one hair went and got stubborn and hid down there in that hole that goes in right where the length of my hair leaves off. Here I am in the rip I feel 'cos I'm a-tugging on one strand of my long hair caught in its pull straight from my behind-me-hole to the tippy-top of my head. The break of my hair pinches a prick from my scalp. I feel a sick tickle in my insides and my tiny hairs stand out away from my skin in a lean towards Stuffy's breath.

Here, with Brother's skin turning into cling-wrap under the efflorescent light of the kitchen, is where I am. Leftover marks up his arm turn from a bruise to a dirty piss stain. He has this rubbery band made out of the same sort of stuff as Stuffy's lips. He has it grasped like a fist around his arm at one end, caught in the bite of his teeth at the other end. I was thinking he was pretty clever and all to go on and make a human sling-shot. Just as I was squinting my eyes to see where the object was that he was gonna sling, Toddo said, "Shit, I missed!" I wasn't gonna go and tell Mother about the word that slipped on out of Toddo's mouth 'cos I was too busy wondering who or what he had missed getting. Maybe it was his words, which Toddo wanted to go on and boomerang off the walls.

Toddo makes fresh marks, lets the red slide down and curve *this-away* and *that-away* over knuckles to rivet and smear the reflection of his face in the knife and *drip-drop* mix in with the tomato he stabs on the cutting board. I wanted to ask if doing that to the tomato made him feel better, 'cos he has his mouth open as if to scream, but the only sound comes from the thud and squush of tomato. Or I could've asked if he wouldn't mind, since he wasn't eating it and all, just pushing the red battered thing down Stuffy's opening. But his voice was quicker than mine and tag, he turned to say something about what others would say as nonsense: "Run before you become." With the tomato seeping through his clenched fingers, I could not open up arms, or get my voice to become spoken: Toddo, Bro, I love. Should I, don't I, I didn't run.

In the In-Sink-Erator, Stuff stuffed all the growls in my mouth when

Toddo thrust what was left of tomato into his throat. That was a good thing. But worse came after, when he shoved the T-bone steak gone rancid right along down with the watery pulp, saying, "Can this thing-a-ma-gig handle a bone?" Surely not after being called such a thing as a 'thing-a-ma-gig', was what I was going to say. But I got sidetracked thinking about how meat had been near cut out of Stuff's diet. No sooner had I thought that when I heard an animal-like growl for meat-eatin'. From the sounds of it, everything around or torn from the bone went down to the pit of Stuff's gut! When Stuff was fed, I held my breath and hid. I snuffled noise that grew out of some inside sore that I feel but don't know where. But I did get to panicking 'cos of what it is I do know. I know that it's not good to eat ground-round raw. Meat not seared, tender as loins after lotion, gets to give a turn to the innards, a torso groove it takes. Not to mention what a lone bone could do: tear, sear, scuff-up, choke-up, ground-down.

Who do you know who can stomach such a thing as the thing we're made of?

Where has Mother gone to that I should not know about anyhow? I only mind her doing a whisper to me when it's a 'what to do' or a 'what not to do.' Her voice seems worn-out from always running after the harsh words that hide from the secret that wants the voice to seek itself quietly. What with her whispering not to listen, her yelling at me for talking quietly to myself, I cannot forget how quick the sound of a *hush* can turn to a scream. But grown-ups can forget. Even Toddo's breath trying to escape through his teeth when he can't help himself say 'Shit!' is a thing oftener than not never noticed by anyone besides me.

Toddo, my Bro', he should mind his own mind then too. When I ask, even in a sound softer than Dad's slippered sneaks, 'Why do I need a bath again?" Mother says, "Never you mind." Mom doesn't have to remind him why I got to go and get clean. T-bone Todd, my Broster, he reminds me what I should do tonight. He says, "Off to the tub for a scrubba with ya." Mom leaves leftover chicken saying to Toddo, "Mind your words in front of her."

I don't mind taking it all off. What I mind is getting in the luke warm of all that wishy water. I mind being naked in the bath. What I mind most is my shivered skin. And how can skin be wet and feel puckered-up dry anyway? How can skin get bumps in water and go smooth in air? Bumps make me feel dirty. Bumps on my legs can only be called the same name as the bumps on his arm. Goose bumps make me think of Brother undoing the band around his arm: bumps that bleed up enough for a band-aid. OK, a little bit of blue-red bled from veins under the cling-film of torn skin.

Bumps on my legs here make me forget how clean I came to get. I try to forget that these pock-like skin-up pockets on my skin here remind me of the cold skin covering the chicken Mother left. I try not to remember that the chicken leg skin and the pink of these bumps on my bone legs are made of the same stuff: stuff that gets torn up.

Chicken skin is what I tried to feed to Stuffy one time, after I was told I should not feed the drain or I'd get 'time out' or worse, 'bed time' – Mom whispering, "Off to the mattress ball with ya." I never got how they made 'going to bed' into a game they called 'the mattress ball.' It's all fun 'n' games for Mother and Father 'cos 'time-out time' to grown-ups is up, not out; 'time-out time' when they go up there, tell 'hush-shs.' It isn't the same time as my 'out time.' They don't need to have Toddo remind them to have another 'should have.'

When Toddo reminds me to do what I should have done, all I can hear is music from the drain. All I can feel is the upside-down ball in my throat's insides. All I can go to is a ball I wrap myself in with my legs tucked up, knees to ribs, head to knees. In 'time-out time,' the four walls of my bedroom become a box and my voice is the jack ready to pop up on a loaded spring to spook myself. The bathroom wall has bumps like skin. But it is not pink. The wall is all in white. White as the line of stuff he, my Bro', snuffs up before he tells me to go and 'get lost.' What I wonder is how he can come and find me if I'm lost. Or is 'get lost' a game with just a hider and no finder – kinda like the Joker card the ladies' pink, curved, fingernails fling aside. Can I have someone on my side or is it me alone trying to find a place I can say is a space I'm lost in?

I should've fed Stuffy the chicken skin. He has to eat after all. I wouldn't have gotten caught if it weren't for the bones that are in us all that are like the tiny T-bone, which is near to being the tinsiest of baby chicken bones that I should not have fed him. But I got caught 'cos Stuffy got greedy. After all, you can't go telling a drain what not to do – what not to do at 'that time' or what to do at 'this time' or that 'this time' is that same thing as 'time' to him. You can't go telling Stuff that he should not go and get uptight and spit-uppish.

He goes so greedy when he grinds what's in him up. Do you know how greedy he had to have gotten to have gone and said what he had said? You want to play pretend. Or even better, we better play 'Operator', or maybe they call it 'Chinese Whispers' where you come from. Even that a game has more than one name goes to show how funny the rules are. I'll make a slick whisper in your ear. You lean over to someone next to close to you there and, *hush-like*, say what it was you thought you heard me say and he will turn to the side and sneak a quick-like say it all over again. The fun in it is that the message, it gets all quirky; it scurries into other mishaps. Well, let's not ruin the fun of it all. Play fair enough though. Rules are rules. Don't pretend to pretend you didn't hear it right.

Here, I'll lend you a little let-on-in with a whisper no one can get a hear of the 'this' or the 'that' it becomes: *Stuff told me that I should feed him the whole baby chicken.*

This time, I tried to tell him he should be nice to the little chicky-bawk tiny bird of a thing with baby wings and skin like real skin but when real skin goes bumpy in water. But I had to whisper to him because I said so, 'cos Mom and Dad should not hear this –

they're not in on this one. This is a 'do not try this at home,' 'assemble at your own risk,' sort-of game. Besides, their talk would stir in on us to not to do the baby talk, to talk all *purportionalistically proper, young lady, you*. Off sides, I'd say to my parents – save it for the next *'shh'* in your game.

But when it was Stuff's turn to listen? Well, with Stuffy being so far down and me in whisper, he couldn't hear. And I got scared. Stuff's tummy was loud in its growl for supper. I could not get down to that hole in him to stuff some more stuff down past his rubber lips. One would not have thought such made-up noise loud enough to wake the grown-ups up there. So I shoved the whole bird-winged, boned-thing right down Stuffy's opening, saying, "Bottoms up," saying, "Silly, silly Stuffy, silly Stuff." What a lot to become of all that little bit of breathless chitter chatter!

Well, I'll tell you, but don't tell on me, Stuffy did not take well to the chicken at all. He got all choked up. He is so down in that hole of his that I could not tell him to go and spit it out – bird bones and all, burp it up. Stuff has manners, whereas I – well, Dad says I sit like a man: all spread out. Mom says, "Don't belch, it's not ladylike." Or worse yet, "Why does a tear run right there? What on earth were you up to tearing your pink, silk pretties?"

I don't mind big sounds once in a while. But this time, Stuff got mad. How grumpy he had to have gotten to have gone and done what I cannot do now – by the heater here, near his heartbeat through bent tubes here under the vents of underground lungs, beneath the ribcage grill-like strips where the bird got stuck in the nowheres of night, so dark down there. How scared he could have gotten.

He did what he should not do. He tried to make noise loud. He forgot how far out of hand 'quiet time' can get. He didn't play by the rules – the rules state that the object is to say the thing quietly to someone in near range of hearing. He got noise to go up enough to get there, up there where Mother and Father were done doing the 'jump up and down' thing on the 'mattress ball.'

But Stuff pretended not to hear nor see their see-saw trick. He played a 'hide and seek' so sneaky like that he snuck a grunt right up through the central heating out the vents into the center of their room. Before they even got to 'quiet time,' Stuff got to get nearer to their out-of-bounds-space than I've even seen, never mind been near enough to pretend not to be there. He started banging on the walls down in that hole of his: *Bang-Bang-Clunker-Unk-Grunt-Grunt-Grind*. Noises sprung up through all Stuff's connected parts: a *bang* from the sink, an unk from the tub drain, a *clunker* from beneath the toilet seat, a *grunt* from the heating vents. Not to mention, the *grind* that even I couldn't point a finger to. Talk about a trick! Well, did you ever know a seeker who could find the source of a sound disguised in hiding?

Near enough to strain my voice above a whisper I said, "Stop making a scene," knowing sound would reach Stuff as strong as Dad's holler only in echo. "Let's make-up that we made-up." I think that is what he heard me say. Problem is, I'd never know what the saying meant to the hearer 'cos my voice came back as a hollow echo that didn't have a word in it. Stuff caught the words before they could reach me and threw back yucky noises I never heard before. Noises with no words sock-hopped around them.

Terrible sounds spoke in more voices than one, as if we were all closing our eyes in the pool playing 'Marco Polo'. Have you ever played that game? That game where the girl who is *it* closes her eyes and calls out "Marco" to the people she's trying to tag who call back "Polo" so as to hint at where it is they are. So if you're *it* you have to try and find the body that goes with the voice that says "Polo." 'Cos you can't open your eyes, the voices leap away from you as soon as you try to touch where they're coming from. Well, listening to Stuffy was like listening to a bad game of 'Marco Polo.' It's like we had to sit out or something. But we couldn't open our eyes, so we couldn't see that *Marco* was giving *Polo* a piggy-back ride. But we could hear *Marco* calling to *Polo* and *Polo* returning with a call that came from above rather than out there in the pool somewhere. So *Marco* never got any closer or any further from catching the voice of the person he was suppose ta tag.

Stuffy's voice carried off and came back. His sounds came up through his throat and thrusted out through the vents in their room. He must have been choking on bones to have gasped like that and to have spooked 'em enough to go and wake Mom and Dad until Dad came down and did the unheard of – did it until Mom up there could hear me cry like a crybaby, cry like I shouldn't.

No, no, never you mind, I got that wrong. Let's play again and I'll sit out a round and go on and skip a turn.

*Ready or not, here I come!*

He was never not ready enough to come and seek me soon or whisper my name. No, I take it back. I call a 'take back.' He doesn't say; he doesn't whisper. He *unks* or rants on or sometimes—but don't dare tell or let on, or time-out-time is a-gonna be a long one – sometimes, he sobs. Out of a nowhere I never knew was there, comes something slick as a leak from the faucet and out-of-tune with his too-loud of a sound like breathing after running fast away.

You'll never know what the next person hears because you don't even know if the person next to you heard you right. So just trust that what comes back to you is near enough to the truth.

*The drains are Stuff's throats; the garbage disposal is his stomach; the pipes are his intestines; the vents are his air pipes; the fire is his heart, the furnace is his lungs and the heat from the heater is his breath.*

In the tub, I can hear Stuff in a call for me to come. Here in the water, I hear him creep up from the drain. His breath makes bubbles. I am reminded of him by my tiny bones trying to get through the bumps of my skin, pop up through the pores and on to the bubbles going down the drain. I try to forget Stuff down there but when the water is let out, his hunger comes back. His thirst gargles water as fast as Toddo guzzles it down in the morning. What is a Mommy to do? How can I go feed Stuffy when Mom's making me sit in this here tub till water turns to the stuff that stinks?

After bath time, I sit right here on the toilet seat. I am near the heater, remember? You should not go and forget where you are. That's how you get lost. I would like to get nearer to the heater but the towel holder goes before me. I should like to be the wall it holds on to. The wall nuzzles up as close to the heater as you can get – so near to the heater that it shares the paint that coats it: ghost-colored gaps of sores and spaces. But let it go before me; let it go before the towel holder-upper. I don't mind 'cos when I am here on the toilet seat, I can hold on to something hung on the towel rack between me and the heater: a towel, a rag, Mom's hung pantyhose, my Bro's sweat-stained tee-shirt.

If Mom comes up here and sees me here naked now, I won't tell her Stuffy's starved. 'Skin and bones' is what I would say if I were to say so. 'Be mindful of the starving,' I could mention. But I can't say what Stuff says to me to tell her because she wouldn't hear of it. And if Toddo comes up here? Well, I can't tell him that Stuffy's stomach growls like that from his drain hole up through to the bathroom drain. I can't say he's so thirsty that he gulped down the tub water I sat in. How can I say to grown-ups that I worry about the water not being clean and all after what I did in it that I should not have done? How can I explain that what was left in me was all I could give to quench his thirst? Just I forgot that the rule, *If it's yellow let it mellow. If it's brown flush it down*, works the other way round with Stuffy. That's how come I don't need to go where I should go – here under the toilet seat, in that hole down there.

I wouldn't have flushed it down there anyhow. Stuffy glugs his water through the irrigation system. The pipes are the same as Stuffy's throats. You cannot go and choke up Stuff like that. That crap would do him in. My leftovers thrown out would clog up his windpipe. Dead skin let loose from soap scum would stop incoming bubbles from clearing the guck in his arteries. His heart would stop its beat. Our heat would stop coming out hot and comfy. When the heat stops, Stuff's air stops. What is a Mother to do? No, what is it a Mother should not do?

If my Mom were playing, I would bend my head near to her to say: *ventilation, bronchiolar tubes, IV, I have to pee, off with the TV, a drain in, adrenaline, a line of heroin, a drain link, chalk smoke, bubbled coke, choke.*

OK. *Sh*, it's OK. We won't play that anymore. There's no rhyme to that reason. Those are Toddo's words. And Toddo's the type of kid to say funny words just so you won't remember them right. But I can't tell them Stuffy's a part of everything here: tubes tied to the tub drain, heater-hole his only way of breathing. The toilet hole – that's another one. That's the one that goes down to a turn in his tummy.

Maybe Mom's not gonna come home. I forgot she was gone. But I would have told her that I was naked here because I should get my hair dry. I gotta get my hair dry after all. Wet hair can do one in, get one sick, and that is not what I should do – go get sick and all. But maybe I should get the wet hair stuck in a knot around Stuff's adam's apple. What a lot of damage a stray hair can do. If you were to pull such hair out of that other hole, you would feel what I would imagine a pig would feel when he's gutted into the pork that's to become our dinner. This is the hole covered, smooth as the animal skin stretched across Toddo's drum, soft as the moccasin of Father's leather slippers, near to the feel the snake felt unslithering its skin to make Mother's purse.

I should not care what I should and should not do 'cos she is not here. My Brother isn't here either. He goes away – well, in a way. When I am near the heater he takes his turn in the bath. That's his little secret: soak the skin loose. Not like Dad. Dad doesn't say secrets. He just knows I won't say to others what is whispered in my ear. Only I know that I should. No, shouldn't, should I? 'Cos anyway, oftener than not, words whispered to me come back to me as a buzz hum or sometimes a silence, which breathes in other noises I myself have never known the names for.

I am nudging nearer to the heater now. Now that no one is down there.

Except Stuff who is not on his best behavior. What with him in a try to get my body down there, I'd rather be alone here than near a meany like Stuff. I should get nearer now. I gotta get near to get all I can get from what comes from the heat. But I can't go and leave him, can I?

Am I near enough to the heater to be within bounds? I got to be in the game but still safe. I don't want to be tagged to 'Freeze' or called to come over and be the 'Red Rover' or tapped on the head with a 'Goose' or worse, chosen to start the game with a 'You're It.' I don't know how to play games where I'm supposed ta get someone. I only know how to play the person who is supposed ta get away from being gotten.

Here on the toilet seat so near the heater, I can hear him breathe. His breath is hot— hotter than when he wants to eat. He could have a fever. But if he's breathing, I know the chicken's wishbone or steak's T-bone alone isn't the thing still in there, where it shouldn't be – boned up near the collar bone past the rubber lips of Stuff's mouth open wide inside. I can flush the toilet without anything of me left in it. That'll fill 'em up, clean 'em out, slide all the way down the hollow of his funnel.

Sometimes, I wonder when I sneak away from bathtime to sit on the rim of the toilet, if he has let himself in – in where Mom says, "Don't touch your dirty girl or ouch-ouch with ya." What if I could hide myself in that hole and turn inside out? Then no one could find me. I would really have won at what my Brother had called the 'go get lost' game.

What about Toddo? What would clog those pores of him pouring open out of every hole in him: his mouth hole, his skin holes, his nose holes, his whole of holes in Toddo! Could I hold Toddo tight as the sling, which strangled his arm, tight as Mamma's lips over his, tight as the band, which made the white of him whiter – braid and wound like the rope he swung from, looped and tied like the mouth hung open in a moan for *Mamma,* open in a circle like the wounds that wind skin to pucker around?

And it isn't just the heat that I want. With the heater comes air blown up fast; with the air comes the noise of the upness, of Stuffy pushing the air out: the *Gurr,* the *Spitter-Spatter,* the *Clunk-Clunk.* With these noises come more noises from deep down these pipes back to the digestive system. But up here, with the heater, there is the sound of his heart trying to beat itself out from under his breath. Here are noises coming from my throat. I am all: *Groan-Growl, Moan, Wah-Wha.*

What without Mother telling me I should not be a crybaby, I cry and cry. I cry to Stuffy through the heater. I shout out that I am too tired to feed him and I don't want to play Mom anymore. But even I know I said it too fast for him to hear. So I whisper to him through the heater that he should go and shut up. He should not be such a crybaby.

Now's the time to suck my breath in and put my hand on my hip and tip myself like a tea-pot to pour myself out into folded wings and to wear myself out in wondering how far I can get this finger in. How tiny I can get when Stuff goes all out in a growl of air, full blown with the hair cleaned out.

Feed me and my Mother Hubbard, I holler into the water between my legs – the water that lets me see that other mouth. I am sticking up myself until something in comes out, until I up-chuck and spew out a few leftovers to flush down for Stuff. Can you puke out of that other mouth? If I go with a finger – in past the curve that dips up, could I, should I, won't I choke?

**Victoria Quinn** was born in England but grew up in Fiji and Hong Kong, where she had an article published in *The South China Evening News*. After graduating from the University of St Andrews in 1990, she worked in publishing before becoming a secondary school teacher and Welfare Coordinator in Cambridge. Now back in St Andrews, and about to start a Ph.D on postcolonialism, she has just finished writing and directing her first film, *The BamBam Club*.

VICTORIA QUINN

# Baba Yaga's Daughter

*LISTEN. Do you want to know a secret? Deep in the forest is a grove of old pines that nudge each other and clatter their black branches when the moon sits fat and white above the mountains. They look like a parliament of crows, or like priests at a bear-baiting who wait to ride the blood. These trees are cold and wicked. In the middle of the grove, guarded by their rough skirts, is a stone. It looks quite ordinary, being pale and rough and the size of your head, but it talks to them at night. It talks to them of Baba Yaga with her house that walks and her wailing walls...*

...I never wanted this, but I was the seventh daughter of the seventh daughter of a seventh son. Knowing came with my blood when I was thirteen. I packed my pot, my knife and a flint for fire, put on my good leather boots and a cape of wolf's fur, and left while they were sleeping. That was when the world was young. Their dust will be blowing under the stars by now.

I walked due North, through the soles of my boots and the skin on my feet. My nails turned blue with the cold, thickening like the icicles hanging from every ridge and tussock. I never bathed – there was no time – and one day I realised the fur that kept me warm had stuck to the mud and the sweat on my back. While I slept, it had put out fine roots that burrowed into my skin. I laughed well that morning.

Upright came hard to me after this, so I bent and knuckled my way along. North. Always North. The air was so sharp it felt like knives slicing and scraping. Each night I fell asleep by a fire, curled nose to tail, and every morning there was a little less of me left. I was being cut free, made ready.

I lost my pot and my flint as I skirted a village. I couldn't turn back to find them, so I followed my own thin shadow. Hunger gnawed at my belly, for food was scarce that winter, and the wild things slept their lives away. Even the berries were shrivelled. Sour and dark as a witch's teat, and I should know, eh? The child should never have been let out alone. It was so plump and sweet that my mouth still floods in remembering. Ten minutes later, all that was left was blood on the snow and one small shoe. I used her fingerbones to pick my teeth. Black, white, red. There were only three colours left in the world.

I walked until North became Here. Where the land ended, the water hissed and boiled, steamed and roiled in a golden stink of sulphur. I ran forward and dived off the high rocks, spinning like a swallow in the mist. The hot salt of the waves scoured the fur from my back. It tore the roots free one by one, and it hurt so much I forgot to breathe. I may even have wept for a time… well, maybe not. Tears have never come easily to such as me. When I managed to pull myself clear, I was raw and pink as a newborn. Hair hung down around me in wet sheets, but I could walk tall again. Upright was easy. When I looked to see my face reflected in a small, still pool, my eyes were old and strange. They used to be brown as peat-water, but now they were yellow like a wolf's. They could see fine unsteady lines of light that covered and connected. A tweak here, a snip there, and the earth was mine.

– *Why are you telling me this?*
– *Before you die?*
– *Perhaps. Well?*
– *Because I must. It's part of the bargain I struck. People still need magic, even magic like mine. Without shadows, who can see the light?*
– *But why me?*
– *You put on foolishness like a cloak because it suits you. You too live half in darkness.*
– *Let me go.*
– *My choice. My decision. I have the power, and I choose…no. Not yet. Sit comfortably. There is bread on the table and water in the jar, so you may eat and drink if you wish. Don't look so worried, the bread is not ground from bones, nor is the water mothers' tears. Listen, Little One, to what I tell you.*

I rose to the top of the cliffs with a flick of my hand. Flying was better than walking, and that's the truth. Easier on the feet. I swore then and there never to walk the woods again. So foolish! I broke that vow over and over. Promises are like pie crusts. Made to be broken. Remember that.

As I flew above the trees, my hair fluttered like a thousand feathers and the sun warmed my skin. The snow was melting. I saw men cutting logs, riding to their lovers, pouring wine down their throats from leather sacks. Always and always the friendship of men, against the women left alone to guard the wattle and daub. Sold from father to husband... Huh! To waste so much power in childbearing and watching from doorways when they could wring life by the neck! I would not be so weak. It is true what people say, child. A little wisdom in a girl's head can be like a maggot in an apple. You need to have lived to be truly wise, and what had I done, me with my wolf's coat? What did I know of living? For me, life was black, white and red. I knew nothing of grey. Oh, but I learned.

The house was waiting for me deep in the woods, surrounded by tall pines. I floated to earth before it like a winged sycamore seed. Gravely, it rose up and bowed. It was a rickety thing, but it stood tall on pale, scaled legs. A bit like a chicken's, but with talons worse than mine. Sitting back down, it watched me through broken eyes. I bowed back. A door opened. I have lived here ever since. We move fast and quiet, taking what we will. Sometimes, we even give. That skull howling over the door was Ivan Pietrovich. He whipped his wife for not giving him a son. Whipped her each night until the blood ran freely from her shoulders, when it was him, him with his rotten seed, that kept her barren! One night, he never came home. I gave her that.

– *Why do you shudder? You, who are neither man nor wife? You think I hunger? Look! I suck eggs now, child, and my strength is failing. I'm still strong enough, mind, to keep you here until I'm done. Don't get any ideas, Little One…and don't try lying. I can read your eyes.*

– *Will you die?*

– *Die? I can't. But I can change. I can run with the wolves again and howl at the moon. Like this. Then, one day, I'll smell her on the wind, and I'll stop a woodsman's spear. He'll give her my skin and I'll take root. Power never dies, Little One.*

– *Why do you keep calling me that?*

– *Why? Why? Why? So many questions. Be still or I shall chop you up for pies. The night is passing and soon you must go free. Make sure you keep the path, there are wolves abroad. Now, listen…*

Those femurs there, tied on to brace the lintel, those I just took. Stupid boy to challenge me. Me, in the fullness of my power! He was young and handsome, but so very, very foolish. I called lightning down upon him as he stood under the tall trees, with his iron sword raised high above his head. We ate well that night, my house and I. Remember, Little One, as you go marching home: there is nothing as rich as the flesh of a good man.

# Seven Days

Day one, he squeezed the rock until it bled.
Wet red seeped through his fingers, plashed and coiled
In clots upon the ground.

Day two, it was more malleable, ready
To be peeled, annealed, spot-welded into shape,
Then plunged in cold water.

Ochre-dusted sheets of stone were laid
Upon the ground in even ranks but, on the third day,
Rose a chink of barbed rebellion.

Day four, the spoil and slag were scraped together.
Thrown on the water, the silt and pumice swayed
To the hitch and pulse of tides.

Now bored and heated by the furnace, on day five,
He made mud pies, breathed life between the grains,
Discarded what began to sprout.

Day six, he took his finest thin, serrated chisel,
Carved links that tied the sea to a land that sulked
Around the margins.

Day seven, the mud pies rose up against him,
Tied him tight against the anvil. Mountains roared,
To watch him chew his bottom lip.

# Sugar & Spice

Take two eyes:
Fill them with water,
Prick out the lashes,
Then put to one side.
They will be baked blind.

Press and roll pale flesh:
Kneaded, it will swell in the heat,
So slice and splice it finely,
Wrap it in cloth and
Leave it to prove in dark places.

Sugar-glaze the lips, child:
The mouth needs to be sweet.
Tip the breasts with honey.
Hair should be caramelised,
So add it later.

When all is cool.

**Christian McLean** was born in New York and still lives there. He received the Charles H. Prize Award for Poetry in 1999, but has turned his attention to short-story writing. He travels extensively and in his spare time enjoys photography and golf.

## CHRISTIAN MCLEAN

# Koi

SOME PEOPLE liked fishing for marlin; others tuna. Anderson liked the Japanese.

"Pound-for-pound they're the best fight in town," Anderson said.

"I don't know, Czechs are pretty intense. Hard to come by, but powerful little teeth on those kids. I grabbed one, must've been three weeks ago in Union Square, dropped him off by the used book people. That kid could bite. Look at this," Damon said. He rolled up his left sleeve. Under his denim jacket and thin cotton sweater, he revealed a wound with a one-and-a half-inch bite-radius. Typical size and depth for a Czech child.

He knew we'd seen worse. Anderson once got involved with a Czech midget when he mistook him for a young boy. The bite was roughly the same size, but the little man's sharp teeth viciously punctured his skin. If it hadn't been for the suit jacket he was wearing, Anderson would be missing a one-and-a half-inch oblate spheroid from his right arm.

It was cool for early September and most people wore light jackets or sweaters. Leaves looked as if they were beginning to dry out and a black woman pushed her daughter on the swings near the pretzel vendor. The little girl giggled and kept yelling *Higher!* Her mother obeyed, adjusting her leather pocketbook straps every two or three pushes.

Anderson was sitting on a bench when we arrived with a sack of Krispy Kreme, coffee, and tea. Damon munched on his raspberry filled donut, getting powdered sugar all over his navy sweater. He looked like a coke addict gone sloppy and I slapped him on the back of the head.

"Look presentable for godsakes," I said.

"What?" he said, his surprise muffled behind a mouthful of jam.

"I've been here since seven," Anderson said.

"Wait, I thought you said we were gonna meet up at nine," I said.

"I did. I was just staking the place out."

"You mean casing the joint."

"Yeah," Anderson said. "I never realized how quiet the park can be early in the morning."

"You get some time for deep reflection and some Zen-Chi?" Damon asked.

"Eat a dick, jelly boy."

We plopped ourselves down next to Anderson giving a certain respect for each other's personal space. The three of us sipped our drinks. Anderson refused my extra donut and by 9:45 the park was moving.

"I saw a guy beating-off two urinals down from me."

"That's gross."

"No shit."

There were two policemen in the park. By noon there would be three or four. The scent of giant soft pretzels in the crisp September air reminded me of high school football games. It smelled like autumn.

Two girls went about their business on the bench across the path. They both wore NYU sweatshirts, one purple, one grey with purple writing. One held a spiral notebook with a golden torch embossed on its red cover. The girl in purple wore tortoiseshell glasses and was reading Kafka. Her friend sat nursing a cancer stick, blowing upward with added force trying not to envelope Tortoiseshell's face with smoke. Each held a Starbucks cup and it made me sick to think about the amount of cash shelled out for coffee when they could have easily put it towards topnotch donuts. Everyone's got their thing I guess.

"Sorry about this morning," Anderson said.

"Forget it," Damon said.

"I didn't know she was going to be in there."

"Well she was, so just drop it."

"Sorry, but I'll make it up to you. I didn't want to tell you before, but I found the lure of lures."

"What are you talking about?" Damon asked.

"Nanji desu ka?"

"What?" I asked.

"You remember a last week when it was pouring out?"

"No."

"Well it was, so I ducked into Barnes & Nobles, you know just to dry off. And I started thumbing the hardbacks in the cooking section for thoughts on dinner."

"And you bought *Chicken Soup for the Soul*, right?" Damon asked.

"Cute. Anyway, I grab some random book. Might have been Martha Stewart, I don't know. But I start flipping through it looking at the pictures and stuff and I stumble on these recipes for Miso Soup and Tempura Shrimp, and it hits me." Anderson paused for effect.

"What does?"

"If you're gonna go for the big game you've gotta have the right bait."

"You think you're gonna catch kids with fried shrimp?" I asked.

"Don't be a moron, it's so unbecoming. I bought the *Idiot's Guide to Japanese*."

"No you didn't?" I said.

"Hell, yeah. Moses didn't leave the Ten Commandments on the mountain, did he? And if you're worried about a paper trail, don't, I paid cash. Anyway, back to the subject. I find this phrase: Nanji desu ka?"

"I know you just said it. What does it mean?" Damon asked.

"What time is it?" Anderson said.

"You got a watch, bitch," Damon said.

"That's what it means."

"I don't think I'm getting it," I said.

"You find a Japanese person and you go up and ask them what time it is and while they're distracted—boom, you snag their kid."

"How are you going to steal their kid if you're asking them what time it is?"

"Smoke-screens, my friends. One of you will ask."

"No, this has always been a one man operation. Two of us watch, keep an eye out for John Law and things of that nature, while the other does his casting," I said.

"I had an epiphany and it was the smoke-screen!"

"Shhh! Not so loud."

We had realized that the first few times were flukes. With no preparation we just went for it. Since then, we had become systematic about things. We all had our jobs, we all had our parks to patrol. Fluking still occurred, usually on the way back from work and generally alone. We did it in our own ponds mostly. Anderson's was Washington Square Park, which he had been casing for the past three months.

"This place is gonna be packed soon," Anderson said.

"Central Park was pretty calm seas this morning," I said.

"It's almost Fall. The season's pretty much on its way out," Anderson said.

"It's a shitty park and it's too small," Damon said.

"Central Park's huge."

"Not Central Park, Union Square. And I don't want to go anymore. I want another park."

"It's on your way to work. Deal with it."

"It's filled with shoeless bums. I lose two bucks in change every time I walk through."

"A. Don't give them change then. And B. If you can find another park that you would rather walk through every day, by all means do it. But until then, pull your weight," Anderson said.

Damon started his second donut while Anderson began to map out the plan of action.

"Generally speaking it's a trolling day," he said. "What we have here is a system of paths all leading to the same spot, the fountain, which means we have to get them before they reach the fountain. Coincidentally, that's going to be our crow's nest."

"We go through this every week," Damon said.

"We've got to cover the variables. So, as I was saying, they seem to be setting something up over there, probably some artsy-fartsies with nothing better to do on a Saturday. Gotta be aware of that. It's a great draw, despite the crap acting. It's not every day you see people acting inside a large fountain. People will be walking down these paths to see what's going on. As much as I hate to say that that's the calibre of attractions New York now offers, it's still a tourist attraction. We have to use that to our advantage. The man on the fountain has to keep in touch, be a spotter. The other will be on the fringe with me, causing the smokescreen."

"No, no, no. I already said no smokescreens."

"But it's crucial to the operation as a whole. If it works here, it could work anywhere. I mean there's a whole section of *Idiot's Guides to Languages*. We can use it everywhere, it could be the thing that leads up to the hotdog hand-off."

"The hand-off's a dream."

"None the less, *we* need, *I* need a smokescreen. I've done the research. I've read the book."

"Then *you* ask the fuckin' question!" Damon said.

Anderson and I looked at Damon. He was watching one of the college girls on the green bench across the way. A red light kept flashing in my head that read *Abort! Abort!* I don't know what Anderson was thinking but I assumed he was beginning to feel that all things weren't hunky-dory with regards to Damon and the mystery woman in his bed this morning.

"Listen, I'm just saying that if you're the one who knows how to speak Japanese, then you should be the one who asks what time it is," Damon said in a calm voice. The light in my head stopped flashing red, and switched to a dim yellow caution, the proper color when trolling.

"You guys don't even like Japanese. I do. Its like if I decided to go to Union Square and snatch a Slovenian."

"Good alliteration."

"When was the last time you saw a Slovenian in Union Square?" Damon asked.

"I haven't, but you get my point. Eastern Europeans are your thing, your Striped Bass. Japanese are mine."

The girl in the purple sweatshirt looked up for a moment, possibly puzzling over Kafka, possibly hearing Anderson say that Japanese were his thing. Of course she would take it out of context and just assume he had a thing for Japanese women. She might even think he was a pervert. It didn't matter as long as she didn't think we were up to anything out of the ordinary.

"Are you gonna learn Czech for me?"

"Sure, I'll learn how to say, 'I'm a Yankee Doodle Dandy' in Archaic Norse if you think it'll add to the haul."

"Seriously?"

Anderson didn't answer. His eyes were intently fixed on a mother and daughter walking down Washington Square North on the outside of the park.

"What's he looking at?" Damon asked.

"A woman. Looks Asian," I said.

"Damn tree," Damon said moving side to side, trying to get a view. "Japanese?"

"Possibly. Just possibly," Anderson said.

The woman was thin, in dark blue denim from head to toe, as was the rage for some unspeakable reason. But was it the rage in Japan? I don't think the *Idiot's Guide* provided anything about style other than kimonos. She entered the park, her daughter trailing slightly behind her in an unzipped yellow down jacket. Our eyes grew larger as the woman and child came past the first set of benches. I scanned from left to right and back to left like I was about to cross a busy intersection. It was clear, except for the two girls across the path from us.

"Anderson," I whispered.

"I know, I know."

"How do you say it?"

"What?"

"She's coming, how do you say it?"

"Nanji desu ka."

"Nanji desu ka? OK."

The little girl's white shoes moved slowly as she trailed farther and farther away from her mother. Anderson was already planning where he was going to release the girl once he snagged her.

"I'll make the drop at the garbage can by the entrance."

"It's dangerous," I said.

"It's gotta be that way. There's no where else to go."

Those two college girls were still sitting across from us. Damon had put his coffee on the ground. I sipped my tea to cover my eyes. *Where are the cops?*

The mother's arms swung with purpose as she walked. I admired her legs which in my book were kind of long for an Asian woman. Maybe she was part German which made her anybody's game. She was wearing narrow boots with three inch heels, not really made for running. Even at the pace she was walking it was apparent that she couldn't go much faster without turning an ankle.

"Nanji desu ka?" I whispered.

"Nanji desu ka?" Anderson repeated.

Damon was watching the two girls on the bench. He looked to our left, down towards the fountain where people were beginning to congregate.

"Cops?"

"Nope."

The girl in the purple sweatshirt closed her book. Her friend lit another cigarette and seemed to be packing her things.

"You see that?" Damon asked.

"Three inch heels," I said.

"No, they're leaving."

Anderson hadn't broken his focus from the child. *Five or six*, I thought, *maybe seven. Japanese kids are kind of on the small side.*

"Go to the fountain," Damon whispered to the girls. "Go to the fountain."

"Nanji desu ka?" I whispered.

"To the fountain."

"Nanji desu ka?"

The mother was almost twenty yards away. Both college girls stood up at the same time and headed towards the fountain.

"Clear on the right," Damon said.

"How do you say 'excuse me'?"

"Shitsurei shimasu."

"Shit-sureish-im-a-su. Seriously?"

"Yes."

"Shitsurei shimasu, nanji desu ka?"

"Sharpen the hooks, gentlemen."

I stood up following the girls towards the fountain. It had to look like I was walking towards the mother and I had to stop her once she passed Anderson. I threw my tea into the garbage can and headed back towards the bench. She had just passed Damon. His nostrils flared as he sniffed her perfume. If Anderson extended his leg, her three inch heels would have tripped over it; she was that close.

"*Nanji desu ka?*" I whispered as I approached. *Make eye contact. If she sees your eyes, she can't see your face.* My heart was in my throat. *Just breathe, nanji de-, nanji de-, shit, shit, Shitsurei shimasu, nanji desu ka? Nice legs, no no no get back on track. Shitsurei shimasu, nanji desu ka? Here she comes. Look at her eyes. Look up lady, for godsakes get your eyes off the pavement.* Anderson started leaning forward. By the street a tall man in a red baseball cap was buying a hotdog. *Here she goes. Eye contact. Keep staring, only five more feet, nice eyes! Control the tension. OK here it is, and three, two, one, speak, now, now damn it!* My mouth opened, she was right in front of me, *Here we go.*

"Mommy, my legs are tired."

*What the hell was that?* Anderson fell back against the bench and Damon's eyes dropped from their alert position to the floor. He had raspberry jam on his shoe.

"We're almost there, honey." The mother turned around and waited until the kid caught up. She stuck out her right hand and the little girl reached her tiny fingers out to her mom. If I wasn't so pissed off, it would have been a beautiful moment worthy of a black and white photograph. They walked hand-in-hand to the fountain where they stood and watched the performance.

It was 2:37 and the play in the fountain sighed its final breath an hour ago. It was a terrible performance of *Macbeth*, placed in the present day. Duncan was the CEO of a multi-conglomerate or something. I walked by once or twice while casing the joint and it was just horrid. Probably a freshman acting class with something to prove. Despite their dull, stuttering blank verse, the day was beautiful. Birds were chirping, the sun was shining, and old Italian men played bocce in the back of the park. They argued in the language of their native country and I kept wondering when someone was going to bring them cappuccino or heaping bowls of pasta.

We never went for Italians on account of my heritage. Belgians, Swiss, Irish, and Scandinavians were also out of the equation, although I had been lobbing that the Scandinavians be removed from the protected species list, because Anderson was only two or three percent. Sure his name might sound as Scandinavian as Valhalla but the fact remains we shouldn't have to sacrifice an entire nation of people just because his first name was the same as the *last* name of some storyteller.

This wasn't a *Fuck you* to Japan either. We weren't nationalist freaks trying to create an isolationist society. It had nothing to do with Pearl Harbor. It was Anderson's thing. He thought they were exhilarating. He said their fight was noble and honorable.

We hadn't seen a single Japanese kid all day. There were some teenagers walking around chattering and I thought to try my newly-discovered linguistic abilities, but then decided to keep that bit of knowledge under wraps. In my head I kept saying it, *Shitsurei shimasu, nanji desu ka?* I mumbled it to a tree when no one else was around. There were sirens in the distance.

To keep in contact we beeped each other with our Nextels and talked like we were Secret Service or Special Ops. soldiers. Anderson was getting antsy. It seemed like every five minutes he beeped in and asked me if I'd seen any. "That's a negative, roger-dodger." I hadn't packed a lunch and I was regretting it. My stomach grumbled and I started eying the vendor by the bathrooms.

"Two hotdogs, sauerkraut, mustard and a bottle of Poland Springs."

He dipped his metal tongs into the old warm water of the cart and placed one dog after another onto the buns. He pumped yellow mustard out of a gallon container and with the same tongs heaped sauerkraut on top. I paid him $4.50 and took my food and water to a bench near the bocce court. Damon walked out of the bathroom and headed past me without looking in my direction.

"Hey," I said. "You see the guy masturbating?" Damon turned around.

"Shit, I didn't even notice you there."

"It's what we in the business like to call *camouflage*."

Damon sat down and whispered, "Yeah, you blend in with all the other fruit loops in Greenwich Village." He added, "Pillow biter," and gave me an elbow.

"Whatever. I'm the one with the beautiful girlfriend. Ya know, humpin' ugly chicks doesn't make you a heterosexual. Just makes you desperate and confused. I've always wondered about you, a little light in the loafers, as they say."

"Anyway back to reality. How long are we going to be here for?"

I took a bite of my hotdog.

"I don't know. Until we catch something. It's a beautiful day. Just sit back and take it all in. Wanna dog?"

"No thanks. You know what they put in those things?"

"Yup," I said and took another bite.

"You got mustard."

"Yeah, mustard and sauerkraut."

"No, on your face, you've got mustard."

"Oh."

Anderson beeped me and asked if I had seen anything worthy of reporting. "Negative," I said. He then beeped Damon who repeated, "Negative."

"He really walked in on you and that girl this morning?"

"He threw the Breton's dog on us and she nearly died."

"Naturally."

"No, I mean seriously. She's like deathly allergic to dog hair. She's in the hospital."

"Jesus. You gonna visit her?"

"You think I should? I mean, if we were making out – not us, but, you know, and some guy you've never seen before walks in the bedroom and throws a dog at you, sending you into anaphylactic shock? I mean would you want to see me again?"

"Depends if you bought dinner."

Anderson beeped in again and we said the same, "Negative." The next time he beeped we swapped phones and confused the hell out of him.

"Fins at ten," Damon said.

"Where are you? Where are you? Ten o'clock, ten o'clock where!"

"Ten o'clock up your ass. Can we go soon?"

I beeped Anderson, interrupting their conversation. "Asian parents and child, possibly Japanese, repeat, possibly Japanese!"

"Where? Where?"

"Ten o'clock."

"Ten o'clock where?"

Ten o'clock up your ass."

"Where are you guys? You're supposed to be keeping watch."

"We are, but this is ridiculous. Repeat ridiculous."

We sat there until 3:46 when Anderson came over and said, "If you guys aren't going to help me."

"Take it easy there, Santiago," Damon said.

"Shitsurei shimasu, nanji des u ka?" I said.

"It's 3:47. Alright, we will stay here 'til 4:00, then call it a day."

"Why don't we call it a day now?"

"Because it's my charter."

"Says who?"

"Buddha," I said.

"Thirteen minutes, twelve minutes now. That's all I'm asking for."

"Fine, fine, fine, but you remember this when we go to Union Square."

We lifted ourselves off the benches and broke out like billiard balls, I took east, Anderson north, and Damon west. We found nothing and reconvened at the fountain, shook hands and made plans to meet up for drinks later. We never fished drunk. I caught the subway uptown to Columbus Circle and grabbed a French kid in the park without effort. I dropped him off at Cleopatra's Needle and exited onto 5th Avenue, stopping at the Met to peruse their collection of Rembrandts.

**Rachel Hollon** is from Louisville, Kentucky. She graduated in May 2001 from Baylor University with a B.F.A. in Theatre Performance. She came to St. Andrews as a Rotary Ambassadorial Scholar.

RACHEL HOLLON

# A Quiet Habitation

GERTRUDE'S EYES adjusted to the rectangle of fluorescent light bulbs and she found herself in the mirror. Her freshly washed face looked pale and folded in resignation. She turned her head from side to side, examining the tight skin pulled over her large cheekbones. The little white slopes descended into two dark valleys of collapsed flesh. She fingered her make up brushes and then began the ritual of painting her face into the contours of someone beautiful.

She could not remember the last time she had been seen. Not looked at, but really seen through the eyes of someone who was interested in something other than her fame. As one of the most respected actresses in New York, she was used to being in the public eye. But the flame around her had cooled. She was expected now, counted on to carry a play, deliver it and drive it home. Increasingly, she found herself expected to help new actors find their way in the theatre world. It was up to her to encourage and provide insight. The burden was effortless; she had done it for so long. Yet she often felt herself merely going through the motions of rehearsing without actually engaging in the process.

Directors hardly even bothered to give her blocking, let alone notes. Especially the new ones, the bright young ones with vision. They must have felt they didn't have the right to confront someone twice, three times their age. She missed the artistic discussions. She missed being doubted and having to prove herself. To no longer have her authority questioned meant she was substantial, but stagnant. It was dismissal with the utmost respect.

When she was younger and the toast of Broadway, her hair had been the color of cherry fire. Edible and untouchable, she used to enter a restaurant and all eyes would inevitably turn towards her. People would hold their breath so as not to disrupt the magical air she walked in. She created her own moving atmosphere, and with every step was both elusive and vital. At the table she would be surrounded by people, some as important as her, some wishing they were, some amazed to find themselves included in a single night of fame. On these evenings she would glaze over, effortless and smiling, and melt into the high-minded chatter.

There were times when she used to sneak out to lunch by herself, disguised under a large hat and reading glasses, and hiding behind a *New York Times*. She would study the room, observe young couples, established couples and the silent elderly men and women who had no choice other than to eat alone. At that time, it was a delight for her not to have to share her observations with the person next to her. She would find zest in being silent and solitary. She relished each gourmet bite knowing that by evening the world would slip back into her manicured hands.

Gertrude calmly finished touching up her eyeliner and examined her work. Up close, it was a nightmare of cosmetic wrinkles for only her viewing. For others it was ten feet away, twenty, seventy, depending on how expensive their tickets were. Her hair rested in well-trained curls, crowning her auburn head with glints of silver. Lipstick, blush and powder were all in place. Her eyes were two ancient black butterflies nestled under the deep shelter of her brow. They opened gently and closed their wings as she pondered her ageing reflection. There was a sharp knock at the door and Gertrude snapped to attention. She detested the intercom system, dismissing it as too impersonal.

"Come in!"

The door opened revealing a youthful frame in the taut stance of a soldier under orders.

"Ms. Roberts, I just wanted to let you know, this is your five minute call."

She surveyed the slick dark hair, took in the pale complexion and fresh cheeks, then focused all of her attention on his eyes. Blue. The directness of her gaze seemed to shock him and he shifted his weight with a nervous smile. Was it John or Joe?

"Alright darling, I'll be right there."

"Thank you, Ms. Roberts." Then as the door closed, "And break a leg."

She hated that expression. The older she got the more she actually feared she might do just that. Gertrude slid a long gray robe onto her shoulders and with it, the weight of the show. She pressed a hand to her temple and floated out of the room. Yes, she could still float.

The quiet black of backstage had always been a temple for her. It was here that she worshipped, here that she found her desired solitude. The theatre was a religion and she one of its high priestesses. Its grandeur captured her spirit, but also offered a simple and familiar focus. She felt singled out, and at the same time returned home: she was once again a little girl sitting in the cozy glow of her parent's kitchen. Her mother baking fresh biscuits, singing along with the radio, with the rising sun as her morning spotlight.

From the sound of things the show seemed to be going well; it was a Saturday night, always the most responsive. People had a full day to unwind from their workweek. They were well fed, dressed up and ready to be entertained. Audiences were like children and had to be treated with the same care and attention. If they were sleepy or didn't want to be there they would let you know with their sulky silence or, worse, their shuffling and coughs. Without fail, if a show was boring, everyone seemed to develop a cold. But when they were happy, when they were absorbed, the entire building would heat up with their excitement, their laughter, and their tears. There was no price for the intoxication a satisfied audience could offer. Applause was merely icing, a toast, a wink, a smile.

Gertrude closed her eyes and allowed the warmth of the air to massage her. She made a silent prayer, forgot herself, and entered, upstage right, down center.

Above her was piercing white, in front a sea of midnight blue and a house full of floating heads. They bobbed and swayed peacefully in a bronze glow. There were dresses of every color and cut, twinkling sequins, velvets, chiffon, grinning bowties, the best of the best. It looked like a hushed cruise-ship party, the Titanic before disaster. In the sea she watched the anxious faces leaning in to find out what would happen next. Others relaxed in what looked like a state of contentment, maybe reflecting on their own youths, reaching for a loved one's hand. She saw whispers and unconscious gestures, tenderness, and insecurity. It was a sea of little dramas playing themselves out. They were a delicious sideshow, a performer's performance.

Gertrude glided around the stage, and met the appropriate cues and gestures. Strong and in control of the scene, she lit a cigarette and reclined onto the chaise longue. It was time for the young ones to confess and for her to appear horrified. Her 'son' and 'his girlfriend' spoke, and Gertrude remembered a time when she had been in a similar situation. She was young. Nineteen or twenty? He had been older by six years, attractive, but not handsome. They had been together for about a year; he had green eyes and their best months were the summer. She remembered his white linen trousers and a night by the lake. Gertrude raised her penciled eyebrows and cocked her head in amusement.

"Well dear, I think your father should hear about this."

It was time for an exit downstage left.

As she rose she felt her robe tug at something. She didn't want to rip the expensive garment and bent down to slip her finger over the fabric. It was caught on a loose screw on the side of the chaise longue. She softly pulled at the material, but it had worked itself into the grooves of the screw. She wasn't going to be able to glide over this one. She sat back down on the couch, and leaned over to release the silk. In front of her the young lovers were arguing in stage whispers. 'Randolph' and 'Sylvia' were about to make their exit before Gertrude could return with his father. It was almost the end of Act One.

Gertrude concentrated on freeing herself. Her fingers fumbled with the fabric. The material had become so entangled in such a short time that the whole thing was becoming slightly comical. Without explanation, she felt her focus drawn upwards. A slight shiver ran through her shoulders. In the back of the auditorium two simple and unapologetic moon-colored eyes stared back at her. Their yellow glow seemed to come from two old-fashioned lamps that someone had forgotten to extinguish. Gertrude sat straight up in response to their call. She felt elongated as if her head floated above her neck. The eyes burned with a steady glow, and when they blinked a corner of the room eclipsed. In their embrace, Gertrude felt all of the things that were true in her come out of a hidden retreat. She imagined a confessional face.

The fabric fell from her hands and she forgot her struggle with the robe. All she heard was a soft persistent hum. It was as if she had dived into a lake in front of her and was plunging deep into the water below. She imagined swimming past all of the beautiful, well-dressed people to the other side where the eyes beckoned her. The pool was thick with memories, and as she swam they clung to her like dead leaves until her body became so heavy that she could no longer move her arms or legs. She was now covered in leaves and being softly pulled down to the lake floor. Gertrude heard the ringing in her ears, felt her body go cold and tingling as her vision blurred into a haze of black and white.

It wasn't until her son discovered she was still on stage, came over and placed his hand on her shoulder that she realized she had been holding her breath. She was leaning forward and all of her weight was on her elbows as if she had been trying to tell the audience a secret.

"Mother, are you feeling well?"

Gertrude looked up into the brown eyes above her, and tried to find one point to focus on. Her 'son' appeared confused. This alarmed her and she felt her cheeks flush. How long had she been sitting like this? Gertrude looked out into the audience. They were waiting for her reply. She managed a weak smile and patted her hair before answering.

"Why, of course dear. I was just resting for a moment." Gertrude gave a little laugh and shrugged her shoulders to assure the actor that everything was under control.

"I see. In that case, you're still going to fetch father aren't you?"

"I'm on my way darling. Don't rush me, I'll get him."

Gertrude reached down and gathered her remaining energy to rip the fabric off the screw. She could feel the eyes burning into her back as she exited.

Back in her dressing room she sat down on her chair, steadied her hands, and once again examined her face in the mirror searching for a clue to what had just happened. Underneath the make-up that had caked into her wrinkles, she was paler than before.

Her mascara had run a little under the heat of the lights and her brow glistened, threatening further downpour.

She looked deep into her own eyes and saw where the black color ran into medium browns twisting into dark blues. They looked like little pits sectioned and gleaming with layers of devoured life. The layers were a shelter that had been woven over many years. They were designed for self-preservation. She blinked and the borders faded into one mass of color. Gertrude listened to the applause coming up through the stage signaling it was time for intermission. She knew that there would be someone coming back to make sure that she was feeling okay and would be able to continue with the show. There were still fifteen minutes left until her next entrance and this time she didn't want to be left alone. She blew her nose into an old handkerchief and waited patiently for a knock at the door.

There were voices down the hallway. 'Randolph' and 'Sylvia' were laughing about something that had happened at the end of the act. Gertrude strained her ears to listen. For a moment she wondered if they were laughing at her. The idea made her panic and so she shifted her thoughts and smiled at whatever they were talking about to include herself in the joke.

Gertrude checked to make sure that her robe was straightened and tied properly around her body. Carefully, she tucked the ripped edge into a fold and pinned it with three miniature bronze safety pins. She would make a 'damage' note for wardrobe after the show.

Footsteps approached her door and passed by quickly on tiptoe. A minute went by and then two more sets of footsteps ran by, muffling their sound as they passed her door. They scurried like cheerful mice frightened only when they had to pass the sleeping cat.

Gertrude knew the opening music for Act Two would be sounding soon. Still no one had come to check on her and she wondered if she had really almost fainted onstage or if she had merely let her mind wander for a moment. This time she decided not to wait until the stage manager came to get her. Instead she took one last glance in the mirror, collected herself, and headed for the door. She would wait backstage with the other actors.

# Ornament

I'm sitting in the Rogano
with the boys, again
invisible and grateful
for the pause.
I fade into the corner.
My hair's a noble mess
and I sway to the talk
of girls and jobs
bumming yet another cigarette.
When the check comes
I try to pay,
pay for *something*.
But my note is brushed away
and I understand the game.
Lowering my eyes, I'll take it back,
casually, when no one is looking.

# Snowfall

I have not known death
but I have known you.
Your shadow follows me.
I live in it, shivering.
Like that empty morning,
I am still mourning.

And so I look for you
in other men,
on summer nights,
in drunken kisses,
exhaustible moments
that taste of nothing.

I listen for your whisper,
words on tiptoe
promising heaven
in the shape of tomorrow.

**Travis Sentell** was born in 1979 in New Orleans, Louisiana. He graduated from Emory University with degrees in Psychology and Religion/Philosophy, and is still not quite sure how he ended up in Scotland doing creative writing. Hoping to pursue a career in something artistic, he spends his free time playing funk music, acting, dancing, and writing. This bio is his chance to give a shout out to all his CW peeps, and he is taking advantage of it. Thanks for everything.

## TRAVIS SENTELL

# Playground

CHUCKY WAS BURYING BARBIE in the sandbox when God showed up. Mrs. Tinsler called everybody over to the back steps to do the meet and greet. Excited at the prospect of a new new kid, Chucky left his beautiful plastic friend crammed upside down in the shifting particles of sand and ran over to be included in the introductions.

"Kids, I'd like you all to meet our new student, God. Everyone say Hi."

"Hi, God," came the droning response.

New kids would feel much more welcome, thought Chucky, if the teachers would just let 'em meet everybody on their own.

Two weeks ago, when he'd gone through the same awkward thirty seconds, that'd been the worst moment of his whole life. Having to stand there silent, looking at all the new faces while they watched him and examined him and talked about him. And then they were all forced to say Hi, even though Chucky could tell that some of them didn't want to. One kid, who Chucky later identified as Steven Whaley, even stuck out his long nasty tongue when Mrs. Tinsler wasn't looking.

Everybody scattered back to what they'd been doing, including Mrs. Tinsler, who walked quickly back into the school and left God alone at the foot of the steps. The twins went back to the swings, Timmy and the gang headed over to resume the heated dodge ball match, Pedro went over to play lifeguard in the sandbox, and Chucky stayed with God. He knew how awkward it was.

"Hi."

"Hi."

"How old are you?"

"Five years old."

"You wanna know how old I am?"

135

"OK."

"I'm six. I had my birthday last week."

"Oh."

"I couldn't really have a party cause I didn't know enough kids to come to it, cause I just got here two weeks ago." Chucky thought for a minute. "But if I did have a party, you coulda come to it."

God rubbed his toe in the dirt and clenched his Hulk Hogan lunchbox a little tighter. Chucky thought harder. "I would've given ya ice cream and cake and stuff too. It woulda been a great party, and you coulda come." He squinted, seeing if that was having any effect on the new kid.

"Thanks," said God, still looking at the dirt.

The two kids stood still, examining the ground between them until the bell rang and everybody ran inside.

Mrs. Tinsler called on Chucky four times that afternoon for four different questions. How do you spell the word that rhymes with mall and is a thing you play with? How many brothers and sisters do you have? What is 5 plus 10? What is your address? B-A-L-L, none, 15, 136 Apple Crescent. The questions weren't hard, but four is a lot of times to call on someone. Chucky always figured that he was being picked on for being the new kid, even after two weeks. Mrs. Tinsler only called on God once, and he was a lot newer than Chucky. She asked him what he thought about life, and he said, "Yes", and then she left him alone and went back to picking on Chucky some more.

Naptime and lunchtime passed as usual. Everyone filed through and got the neat poofy blue fold-out mats while Chucky had to settle for the red mat with the holes in it 'cause he was last in line again. The other kids probably thought he didn't know that the blue ones were better. But he did know. He just couldn't show 'em 'cause he didn't get to pick first. It wasn't fair.

"Do you wanna trade food?" asked Chucky at lunchtime. Kids never traded food with him. Even though he liked everything his mom gave him, he thought it would be much more fun to trade. It wouldn't matter if he got something worse, such as a carrot.

"Why?" said God.

"I'll give you my Twinkie," said Chucky.

"OK," said God. "I like Twinkies."

The end-of-school bell finally rang, and everyone went to their cubby holes to get their lunch boxes and backpacks. Chucky had to wait behind Lenora Carver, who always took way too long and always smelled like pee. He didn't even have his own cubby hole, 'cause all of 'em were assigned by the time he joined the class – so he had to share a box with stupid Lenora Carver. No one talked to Lenora that much. Chucky didn't want to either, but she smiled at him sometimes, so he guessed that meant she was pretty nice.

God had to share a cubby hole too, 'cause he was new, and he was stuck with mean Steven Whaley. Steven took an extra long time getting all of his stuff down, and then ran into God on the way out. Chucky was pretty sure that Steven did it on purpose, but he didn't say anything out loud. Steven had a big bruise on the side of his neck, and Chucky heard somewhere that he got it in a fight with a third grader.

Chucky and God walked out of the room together, past Mrs. Tinsler's flowered skirt and tapping foot. The door closed and locked behind them as they made their way towards the front of the school. Chucky was walking extra slow 'cause he figured he should think of something to say. God looked at the floor and wrapped one hand around each strap of his Transformers backpack.

"Is your mom gonna pick you up?" asked Chucky.

"No. I'm gonna walk home," said God.

"Oh."

Chucky had never met someone who was allowed to walk home on their own before. He tried to think of something else to say.

"Do you like ice cream?" asked Chucky.

"Yeah," said God.

"Well, sometime, maybe you can come over and have some. My mom makes a lot of ice cream for me all the time and it's good. It has big pieces of candy in it. You can't have a lot, 'cause it makes your teeth bad, I mean that's what my mom says, but you can still have some, and I bet you'll like it. I like it and it's good." They were at the front door. God pushed the metal bar and stepped into the sunlight. Chucky followed silently, putting his hands in his pockets.

When they got to the carpool circle, God turned around, squinting.

"Bye."

Chucky stuck out his hand like his dad always did, and smiled. "Bye, God. I'll see you tomorrow, and I can talk to my mom, and maybe you can come over and play with me sometime. I have three new Thunder Cats that are really cool."

God gave a half smile and pushed a big piece of brown hair out of his eyes. "OK. That sounds fun."

Chucky watched as God walked down towards the street, stopping carefully at the intersection to look both ways. His Transformers backpack bounced a little with each step, and Megatron seemed to be waving goodbye to the school and all the kids. Chucky sorta waved back, pulled the straps on his own bag tight around his shoulders, and went over to sit in his usual mom-waiting spot. The other kids were playing tag near the covered carpool bench, but Chucky didn't feel like joining them. It was really hot and he was already getting wet arms and a wet butt. He decided to build a little dirt castle for any homeless ants that might come along and needed a place to stay. He kept expanding the dirt mansion, ignoring the screams of the other happy children until his mom showed up to take him home.

That night at dinner, Chucky clenched a fork in his balled-up fist and told his mom and dad all about his new friend.

"That's great, kiddo," said Chucky's dad.

"We're proud of you, son," said Chucky's mom.

Chucky was really happy in his inside parts. He smiled.

"So you gonna have this kid come over here?" asked Chucky's dad.

"Harold!" said Chucky's mom.

"What, honey? I was just askin the kid if he was gonna bring his little friend over."

"Chucky will bring his friends over when he wants to. Chucky, you can have a friend over whenever you want, to play games or eat ice cream—even on school days, OK?"

"I know mom," said Chucky as he shovelled peas into his mouth. "Like a birthday party, only with no cake and no presents, right?"

"You got it." His mom winked. "Now, eat your potatoes if you want dessert."

Chucky had been trying the whole week to find a friend to come over, but even smelly Lenora said she wasn't sure she could come. And Chucky didn't want to ask anyone a second time, 'cause the kids might make fun of him. He wanted to show his parents that he could have lots of friends. Lots of friends different from them. He still liked his parents, but different kinds of friends are good, thought Chucky. And now that God was around, he had a bestest friend that he could hang out with all the time.

The next morning, Chucky was up bright and early, even before his mom came in to wake him. When she finally did come, which seemed like hours and hours later, Chucky pretended to be asleep. Then, when he heard his mom lean over to wake him up with a kiss on the cheek, he opened his eyes and stuck out his tongue. They both laughed, and his mom gave him a big hug and smiled that smile that she gave sometimes when she was sad and happy at the same time.

He ate his breakfast as fast as he could, and laughed when his dad called him a "vacuum cleaner face", because he used to be afraid of vacuum cleaners, but now that he was a big boy, he wasn't scared any more. Besides, he knew that he was faster than any old vacuum cleaner. His dad was pretty funny in a dad sort of way.

Chucky looked in his closet real carefully and finally chose his long pink and black striped shorts and his purple shirt. His hair was spiky in front, and long in the back, and his mom helped him get it just right before she told him to get into the back seat of the car. He tied and retied his shoes the whole way to school.

There were a bunch of kids playing jump rope and dodge ball when Chucky got dropped off. He hugged and kissed his mom. He told her he loved her, and then got out of the car to look for God. It was sprinkling as Chucky walked over to the front doors of the school, and it was raining pretty hard by the time the first bell rang. When everybody came into the class, Mrs. Tinsler was pretty mad because all the books and the floor and the desks got wet. Timmy Perkins kept bending over and shaking his head like a dog in front of Miranda Shala, who screamed every time the water touched her because she was wearing a new lacy dress. Mrs. Tinsler grabbed Timmy by the arm and made him stand in the corner, and also wrote his name on the board in big, white letters. That pretty much made most of the other kids sit down and behave. God was already sitting quietly in his seat at the back of the room, looking out the window. Seating was alphabetical, but since Chucky and God both joined the class late, they got to sit next to each other in the back row.

That's how it should be with best friends, Chucky thought as he slid into his desk. He was extra careful not to shake water anywhere as he sat—his name hadn't been on the board once in the two weeks since he'd arrived at MiddleBrook, and he wasn't planning on changing that now. He opened his desk and hid behind it while he put his pencils away, whispering quickly to God while Mrs. Tinsler couldn't see him talking out of turn. She was pretty busy with the twins right then anyway.

"Hey, God."

"Hi."

"What'd you do yesterday?"

"Went home and thought about some stuff."

"Oh."

There was a pause while Chucky put the rest of the pencils in his desk and concentrated hard on what he should say next.

"What'd you do yesterday, Chucky?" asked God.

Chucky smiled and let some air out of his mouth. "I went home and took a bath and then watched Thunder Cats on TV and had dinner with my mom and dad and then got into bed. My dad read me a story. Ummm…and that's it."

"Do you have nice parents?"

"Oh yeah, they get me presents all the time, and they let me have some of their candy bars sometimes, and my dad is really funny and has a beard. I like them a lot."

The corners of God's mouth crinkled. "What's your favorite thing in the world?"

"In the whole world?"

"Yes."

That was a really hard question. There were bouncy balls, cakes, his parents, Thunder Cats, whirlpools, piles of leaves, his grandpa, Mrs. Wilcox's dog, Uncle Johnny's waterbed, playing football with his dad, dancing around with his mom to the radio—lots and lots of things. What was the most fun?

"My favorite thing, or the most fun thing?"

God thought for a second. "Isn't that the same?"

"Yeah, I guess so."

"Okay, so both then."

Chucky thought hard. Mrs. Tinsler had four people in the corner now.

"Okay, I got it. My favorite thing in the world is fun."

"Your favorite thing is fun?"

"Yeah, cause when I'm having fun, that's when I'm happiest. If there wasn't any fun, then I wouldn't be as happy."

God chewed on the inside of his cheek and brought his eyebrows closer together. "I guess I meant what thing was your favorite, but I guess fun is a thing, cause someone had to invent it, right?"

"What does invent mean?" asked Chucky.

"Like when you make something," said God.

"Oh," said Chucky. "Yeah."

"So fun is your favorite thing in the world?"

"Yeah, I wanna have fun all the time. It's the best. And when I'm sad is my least favorite thing. I don't like to do things that make me sad, like when I do something to make my mom sad. That makes me sad, y'know?"

God scrunched up his face real small like he was trying to poo.

"What's wrong?" asked Chucky.

"I just thought people had favorite things, not favorite...*stuffs*."

"Oh, oh, I can think of a better thing, a better *stuff*, if you want. I just thought that fun and sad things were things too, right? Like things that make you sad is a thing, a *stuff*, right? And you said in the whole world, so that's it, I think."

God's face was still scrunched. "I guess so...I just thought it would be different. I'll think about it. It's OK."

"Chucky! Stop talking right this minute or you will get your name on the board!" screamed Mrs. Tinsler. The kids jumped in their seats at the loud outburst. Her face was red, and she had a lot of small hairs falling around it from her bun. Chucky wanted to tell her that he hadn't been talking, that it had been God, but then he thought that might make him a bad friend, so he kept his mouth shut. The tears started welling up in his eyes, but he fought them down and just stared at his desk. Out of the corner of his eye, he could see God looking over at him gratefully. Mrs. Tinsler should pay better attention, thought Chucky. He'd have to be extra good the rest of the day so he didn't get his name on the board. His mom would be mad at him for sure if that happened, and that would make him sad.

Math was the morning lesson that day, and Chucky struggled in silence to add bunches of numbers together. Mrs. Tinsler didn't call on him once that day, and Chucky worried that maybe it was because she didn't like him any more after she caught him talking. But it wasn't even his fault, it was God's. It wasn't his fault that their voices sounded the same.

"Nicholas! Go write your name on the board!"

Chucky wondered why Mrs. Tinsler didn't like some kids as much as others. Grown-ups shouldn't do that. His parents liked him, but they had to, it was their job. Lots of times, other grown-ups weren't very nice.

"Class! Please! Now quiet down and open at page 47!"

At recess, Chucky went over right away to join the dodge ball game and left God sitting by himself against the brick wall of the school. He didn't feel like talking to God, and besides, he'd probably only get in trouble if he did.

Timmy and Steven were dodge ball captains. Chucky had only played dodge ball once in the two weeks he'd been at the school, and he'd been hit in the stomach really hard and had to stop playing. He still remembered the stomachache and the embarrassment of leaving recess and having to visit the school nurse on only his second day there. So he'd stayed away since that first time, but now he felt like he ought to try again. He ought to at least try to talk with the other kids in his class.

Mike and Rob, the twins, were picked first. They always were. Then Suzy because she was really fast and small, so she hardly ever got hit. Then Perry, and Pedro, and Amit, and Bobby, and Chrissy, and Helen, and then Nicholas (because he wore glasses) and then it was down to Chucky and Lenora Carver. Timmy screwed up his face to choose, and Chucky tried his best to look like he didn't care. He straightened himself up a little taller to make his stomach seem tinier than it was, and moved a little ahead of Lenora. Timmy said, "We'll take Lenora, and you guys can have Chunky." There were snickers from everyone around, especially from Timmy's team. Lenora looked at Chucky and shrugged her shoulders a little bit to show that it wasn't her fault before walking over to join Timmy's team. Chucky looked back towards God, and saw him watching intently. Chucky decided that he was gonna play really hard and get even with all the kids, and maybe God would want to be friends with him even more.

The game started, and Chucky ran really really fast up and down the field to get away from the sharp eye of Steven Whaley, who seemed to be throwing every ball in Chucky's direction. Chucky had a lot to think about. The rain had stopped, but it had left mud puddles all over the big field where the kids played their recess games. His mom would be really mad if he came home with mud on his shorts, or with wet, brown socks. The other kids were running straight through the puddles without worrying about their clothes. It wasn't fair at all, 'cause there were only three or four spots on the field that were still hard grass and not gross mushiness. The ball whizzed by and splattered muddy water droplets all over Chucky's face. He crammed his eyes shut and ran in the opposite direction, back to the safe space for his team. There was only one ball on the field, but it seemed like ten of them.

Chucky stood behind the people on his team for a second, trying to catch his breath. He rolled up his fists real tight, and tried his best to look brave. He could feel the cowlick that his mom always tried to press down fighting against gravity. Chucky stood up straighter and closed his mouth, knowing that made him look tougher. Inside his head, he growled like a tiger. This was where he proved to the other kids that he was good enough to play dodge ball with them, even if he didn't want to. He could have more than one friend if he tried hard. He could show everybody.

The ball came flying past the group, and Chucky turned to run after it. He could feel his stomach juggling and gurgling as he ran, the wind whipping past his ears. Water splashed up on his socks and shorts, but he didn't care any longer. He was gonna get that ball and he was gonna hit Steven Whaley with it. Chucky got to the ball at the same time as Lenora Carver, and they both grabbed it. Chucky wrapped his right arm around it and pulled, so that his elbow went straight into Lenora's chest. She let go in surprise and Chucky felt a rush of pleasure as she squealed in pain. I bet they wish they would've picked me instead of pee-pee girl, he thought as he turned around to face the field. Steven Whaley was standing in the middle of a big mud puddle, hands on his hips, staring at the ball. He was chewing bubble gum. Chucky held the red rubber tightly between his two hands so they wouldn't shake as much from the cold outside. He could feel the little grooves of the ball under his palms, and under his right pointer finger, Chucky could feel the hard black rubber part of the ball where you put the air into it. He rubbed his finger over this little bump as he stepped slowly towards Steven Whaley.

Steven laughed, and yelled loudly, "Hey, everybody, look out! Chunky's gonna do a cannonball in the puddle and make us all drown!"

As the laughter reached his ears, Chucky wiped the water from his eyebrows and dried his hands on the side of his new purple shirt as best he could. The other kids backed off as he approached.

Steven Whaley still hadn't moved an inch. "You and me, Chunky."

"My n-name is Chucky, you, you stupid Steven Whaley."

The crowd of kids were making a circle now, and they all gave an appreciative "Ooooohhh" at Chucky's harsh words. They looked to Steven to say something back.

Steven took a step forward, his Nike shoes sloshing through the dark waters that he stood on.

"If I'm so stupid, Chunky Chucky, then why can't you hit me with the ball?"

The kids looked to Chucky to throw the ball. Chucky started breathing faster, and glanced over his shoulder to where God was still sitting against the brick wall. He was staring straight at the ball gripped between Chucky's hands. God was crying.

Chucky turned back to Steven Whaley, and thought, I'm not gonna cry. I'm gonna knock Steven Whaley with this ball. I'm gonna knock stupid Steven Whaley with this ball in his stupid face. With a cry that was loud enough to make the crowd of kids jump back, Chucky squeezed the ball tightly and rushed forward, bringing it high up over his head. Steven Whaley took another step towards Chucky, bending his knees.

Chucky threw the ball as hard as he could right at Steven Whaley's freckled head. The kids watched with gaping mouths as the red ball flew across the field. A lightning bolt split the sky, and Steven Whaley caught the ball with a rubbery thump, ejecting Chucky from the game. In one fluid motion, the ball was out of Steven Whaley's hands, and back into the air. Chucky watched in slow-motion desperation as the ball sailed back at him. Already off balance from his massive throwing effort of only a few seconds before, Chucky pinwheeled his arms wildly, trying to work up enough momentum to move away from the deadly ball—to get ejected twice in a matter of seconds in front of all the kids would be too much. No one ever gets out twice in the same game. He heard the thunderclap rumble the air as the ball struck him squarely in the face, knocking him onto his back.

Water, laughter, pain, hands covering his forehead where the ball had hit, muddy shorts, dripping hair, ruined purple shirt, more laughter, welling tears…Chucky lay on his back in a puddle of mud as the rain started up again. Mrs. Tinsler, covering her head with a newspaper, rushed outside to call the students in, and everyone hurried back to the classroom as fast as they could. Mrs. Tinsler was already in a bad mood, and no one wanted to push that any farther. The rumor was that she'd spanked a kid with a ruler last year.

Chucky lay on his back, letting the rain drop down into his open mouth. Tears spilled over his eyes, cutting muddy paths across his cheeks before mixing with the brown waters beneath him. His fists were clenched as tight as they would go beneath the surface of the puddle. He could feel the sobs starting up, and he tried to not let them out, he tried to stop himself from crying harder, but he couldn't. He opened his quivering lips and let out a wracking sob. He lay on his back, crammed his eyes shut, and just let himself cry. Rain splashed his face harder and harder, washing away his tears as fast as he could make them.

Chucky felt the rain stop abruptly and opened his eyes. He saw God leaning over his face, blocking the storm. Water was trickling down the edges of God's cheeks and plastering the hair to the side of his face. Chucky could see that God was still crying. The two boys looked at each other.

Another clap of thunder broke the rain-drenched silence.

"Why did you lie to me?" asked God as the tears and rain streamed across his lips.

Chucky stared up at him, unable to answer.

**Amy Woolford** grew up in Dorset. She studied English and French at Queen's University, Belfast, spending a year in France as a teaching assistant and working in an automaton museum. While at university, Amy wrote for the student newspaper and spent six weeks on her local newspaper. Before coming to St Andrews, Amy was a school secretary for two years, a barmaid in her local pub, and an assistant to the village wedding photographer.

AMY WOOLFORD

# Wednesday

I TOLD HIM, I said, 'Look, on Wednesday, I won't be here.' Of course, I was. I came in on Wednesday, expecting one of Steve's witty comments, and he didn't say anything. He handed me my pinny, and that was that. But I knew I was leaving somehow. I wish I could add *anyhow* in there too, but if that had been true I would've already gone. I didn't have the courage for anything like that.

It was my Uncle Gordy who made me so determined to leave. Well, he wasn't really my uncle. I mean, I'm sure you've heard this a hundred times before — he was my mum's bloke, for a while, when I was little. He made me a mobile to go over my bed, with little wooden boats hanging from it. 'Kitty,' he said, 'one day you will sail right out of this dump.'

Thing is, it's not really a dump. Or if it is, it's a beautiful one. Sometimes on my day off, I would get up at the crack of dawn and head down to the shore, just three minutes walk from my house. Sitting on the shingles, watching the sun come up and listening to the sea rush in and out. Now that was nice. But, an hour later, I'd get up, dust myself off, and that would be my day. There wasn't anything else to do afterwards.

Anyway, like I said, I'd promised myself that sooner or later, I was out of there. And it was on that Wednesday my ship finally came in, so to speak.

"All day coffee doesn't mean you have to stay here all day," I said.

I don't know why I ever bothered to say that. Really, Mike and Terry *were* the café. Small square tables, bright easy-wipe tablecloths, chipped white vases with a single wilted daisy in each one — and, of course, Mike and Terry. How nice it would be, I used to say to them, to meet some *new* people, and then I'd sigh dramatically.

So there I was, on a damp weekday morning, suggesting to the two of them that they might like to actually try setting foot in the outside world.

"Steve lets us stay here as long as we like." That was Terry.

"Oh, Steve's so wonderful!"

"He's standing behind you n'all." That was Mike.

"I was just saying how wonderful you are, Steve."

"I heard. The three that have just come in want serving."

I walked over, serving-smile firmly in place. "So, gents, what can I do you for?"

"I can think of a few things!" And *that*, I later discovered, was Frank. He was, at any rate, new people.

"OK, let me rephrase that, what would you like to eat?"

Two fairly hefty guys they were, the father and son. If I remember rightly, they polished off two all-day breakfasts each. Jake, the third guy, didn't — he was presumably too busy being deep and thoughtful, even then. He was twenty, just like me, and a slimmer build than the others, tall and gangly. I think he had a bacon sarnie.

They stayed all afternoon. I got chatting to them, asked them what they did for a living, and how the hell they'd ended up here. They asked me the usual questions. Did I live locally, what did I do outside of work, and did I enjoy my job? That last one was probably a Jake question and it kind of answered itself since Steve kept yelling from the kitchen. We talked about the town. That didn't take very long. I expect we also made some glib comments about politics and the state of the economy.

And that's how it started. That's basically how I got to know them. They had come to build a new seawall, so they rented out a holiday cottage on the harbour and a little boat in it. It was the beginning of a beautiful summer and we used to hang out together as often as possible. Frank, Sam, Jake, and me.

"Sam, we need some more beers out here!"

"You know, you could sometimes get the beer yourself," I said as Sam flung a beer in Frank's direction and placed another three on the deck. The sun was just slipping below the horizon and jagged clouds glowed pink in its wake. A plane droned across the sky, trailing an orange gash behind it. I lay on my back, staring up at the circling seagulls. Frank sat leaning over his knees beside me, looking out across the harbour. Jake was further back, lying propped up against the side of the boat, and Sam hopped about 'making good', though he didn't really know what he was doing.

It was a doddery old boat, peeling a bit at the edges. But there was enough space at the front to lie out in the sun and a cosy nook-and-cranny cabin, so it suited us just fine. Half the time we wouldn't even leave the harbour. Our mooring was in the quietest corner and no-one really bothered us. We liked chilling out amidst the jostling skeleton of criss-crossed masts that filled the harbour, and watching the real boats come in, the big-sea smell of fish floating in with them.

"Sam, you're rocking the damn boat."

"Sorry, Dad."

Poor Sam, always getting into trouble. He seemed to have a knack for it, even if he kept to himself. He was so meek and unassuming, he reminded me of the daisies in the café, sad and a bit wilted.

"Can't you sit still for five minutes?" Frank said.

Sam was still lumbering about the boat. "And do what?"

"Something that doesn't involve moving." There was a pause. Sam was now standing motionless. Frank said, "C'm 'ere Sam, we'll play a few hands of cards then."

Moving over to join his father, Sam sat down beside him. It was never a question with Frank. He never asked Sam what he wanted to do. I guess it wouldn't have made much difference if he had.

"Cards, Kitty?" Frank asked, "Jake, you in?"

I got to my feet, light-headed and crumpled. "No ta. I think I'll take a walk. It's about time I did something vaguely active."

"I'll join you," Jake said, looking over at me and then standing up and shaking himself down. "What new wonder shall we visit today?"

"I hardly know which one to suggest," I said. We climbed the ladder up to the quay and set off towards the cliffs as usual.

Those lazy walks along the headland or along the shore, they were probably my favourite times back then. Jake and I would talk about everything, you know, like when you've talked so much you can hardly remember which bit was their story and which bit was yours. Or we'd find a grassy patch at the top of the cliffs and dangle our legs over the edge, which Jake said was dangerous until I made chicken noises at him. We'd lie back with our eyes closed, letting the sun seep into our skin, and listen to the quietness up there. We could hear the sounds of birds and the sea sighing to itself, but it all seemed so far away, like another world.

On those days, I think I was actually happy to stay put in that tiny town. That whole summer was pretty good. The four of us lounging around on the boat or, if we were feeling more energetic, playing Frisbee or something in the nearby fields. Although Sam was quiet, the other two weren't, and God knows I'm not. There was a lot of laughing, teasing, mickey-taking, that sort of thing. Jake knew about a thousand jokes and under many a clear star-scattered sky, we'd sit around drinking and laughing at Jake, and his jokes of course.

But it was Frank who had the liveliest sense of humour, or that's how it seemed at the time. He'd always be playing these practical jokes. But they were mostly at Sam's expense and I can see now that actually some of them weren't very funny at all. Frank always went a bit too far. Perhaps if I'd paid more attention, I would've noticed that about him. But the rest of the time things were great. Frank was the one, being the oldest I suppose, who kind of took charge and looked out for us all. Some evenings, he would set up a barbecue on the beach and we'd eat hotdogs and burgers and pretty much anything that Frank decided could be eaten char-grilled. It was like a scene from a picture book, sitting on the sand under a huge smudgy blue sky, listening to the sea, tame and calm for once, and to the raucous seagulls squabbling over a bit of burger bun.

Eventually, though, things began to change. 'Change is part of life,' my mother always said. I guess that was because she changed her blokes more often than her underwear. Though it was probably the only thing that did change in that nowhere town. That summer, I think the change started the day we took the boat round to Horseshoe Bay. We moored in the tiny harbour and headed down to the beach. We had martinis for breakfast, crunchy sandy sandwiches for lunch, and a pub supper. We spent the day sprawled out on the beach with magazines and newspapers, fighting over the sports sections. In the evening, Frank and Sam, suffering from varying degrees of sunstroke, headed back to the boat. Jake and I wandered barefoot along the deserted shore, splashing through the white lace ripples. We stopped in the shadow of the cliffs to watch for shooting stars and I just leant back against him and rested my head on his shoulder. He bent his head down close to my ear and whispered something, I don't really remember what, and then he was turning me round to face him and then he kissed me.

I broke away from him. "I can't do this."

He took a step back, his dark eyes wide with confusion. "Why not?"

I scratched my bare arm. "Because."

He looked angry, but most of all he looked hurt.

I turned and ran towards the harbour.

When I got to the boat, I was in some state. Hair flying everywhere, out of breath, and I'd dropped my sandals on the beach. I was crying by then too. Frank was sitting on the deck, smoking a cigar.

"Kitty, what the hell's wrong?"

But I didn't have to say anything. He stood up as I climbed on board and just gave me this big bear hug, strong and safe, and right somehow. That's what it was. It felt right.

And I can't help thinking about that evening now. I roll it over in my mind like a Rubick's cube in my hands, trying to make sense of it, as I wait for Jake. He rang me the other night. He said he'd got my number from a mutual friend. Wondered how I was. Did

I want to meet for a drink? Well, of course, I said No, to begin with. But then I got curious. I wanted to know how things might've been if...well, if things had turned out different. I think mostly, though, I just wanted to see him. After all, it has been nearly two years since that summer, and it didn't end very well between me and him. So now I'm sitting here, fiddling with my glass and trying to arrange my hair further forward over my face. And I see a tall, lean figure walk past the window.

I stand up as he comes over to my table. "Hi," I say. I put out my hand but he leans over and kisses me on the cheek.

"Hi yourself," he says, straightening up. "Do you want a drink?"

"I've got one." I tap my glass of white wine.

He nods and heads to the bar. It's one of those old-fashioned pubs with dark wood-effect beams, probably plaster of Paris, and ye olde photographs on the wall. Several suits stand round the bar perfecting their loud laughs.

Jake comes back, spilling a trail of beer across the carpet. He plonks his pint onto the table and himself onto a stool. We sit in silence.

"How are you?" he says at last.

"Fine, fine. You?"

"I'm good. So what news from the Big Smoke? Is city life treating you well?"

"Yes, it's fine, but I'd hardly call it the Big Smoke." I try to laugh but it's more of a croak.

"I bet you've got a nice big house though."

"Yeah, with a pool." I shrug. "But what's the news with you? What are you up to these days?"

"I've just moved back to the area. I'm working for that construction firm by the brewery. The one that's just started up."

"The rivals, huh? Frank wouldn't like that! Bet they don't pay as well."

"I do okay," he says. "Is Sam still working for his dad?"

"He moved out a while back."

"Hear much from him?"

"Poor Frank, he never gets so much as a postcard from him."

Jake had been absently flipping a beer mat but now he looks up at me sharply. My gaze slides off him and onto the floor.

"Any little Franks running around?" he asks and I meet his eyes this time.

"No." Did I say that too quickly? "You? Is there a Mrs Symonds?"

"No." Did he say that too quickly? "One knock back was enough for me." That was too quick.

I smile sadly, and probably apologetically, which he'll hate.

"Why *Frank*, Kitty?" he says.

Our drinks sit untouched on the table.

"I told you," I say quietly. "Because I loved you, I didn't love him."

Jake twists away from me slightly in his seat. He doesn't want to hear it. I don't want to tell it. But I say it anyway, willing him to understand, repeating the reasons again to myself.

"I needed a relationship I could predict," I say, "one where my emotions weren't involved. Once you put feelings into the equation, there's way more chance it's all going to blow up in your face. I couldn't take the risk. Once I got out of that place, there was no going back with my tail between my legs. Not to that town. Not to my mum and her latest boyfriend. Not to that end-of-the-world, lie-down-and-die resort. It was make or break for me."

Jake suddenly stretches his arm across the table towards me.

I flinch. But he isn't Frank. Maybe I should pull away. I don't.

He puts his hand under my hair and brushes it away from my face, revealing the dark purple blush on my cheek that the make-up couldn't hide.

"And bruises are better than all of that?" Jake says.

He lets my hair fall across my cheek again and rests his arm on the table. He waits for my answer.

"What choice do I have?"

"You have every choice!" he snaps.

I think he's going to continue, but he doesn't. I study a row of sepia family shots on the wall. When I turn back to him, Jake is standing up, his car keys in his hand.

"You haven't drunk your beer," I say.

"And you haven't changed."

Then, as he starts to leave, he says, "What would your Uncle Gordy say if he could see you now?"

Born in Cumbria in 1979, **Mark Langwith** has lived there in the Lake District all his life apart from five years at St Andrews where he graduated with a First in English and Modern History in 2001. At first interested mainly in poetry, he has developed a taste for short stories. In September 2002 he will begin researching J.R.R. Tolkien for a Ph.D at St Andrews.

MARK LANGWITH

# The Church Roof

HER DAD SAID that God was crying. It was the first week of August, the middle of the summer holidays. The rain had started on Sunday and hadn't stopped.

When it had rained for some days, she had asked her dad whether their house might be washed away. He said that some people built their houses on sand, but that theirs was built on stone. Their house was built *of* stone, too, and stood alone among open fields. It had a garden with a small stream near the far end crossed by a tiny humpback bridge.

Through her bedroom window upstairs, which was flecked and streaked with rain, she could see the fringes of a waterscape in the surrounding fields. Beyond that the rain smudged everything into a grey pastel nothing. Below her she could see the raindrops bouncing off the little glass greenhouse where her mum used to grow tomatoes. One year the Pest had got them. Her mum had said the Pest lived under the little wooden bridge. Her mum had also grown flowers which were yellow in the centre with white tips. They were called 'fried-eggs'. They had all gone.

The stream had burst its banks on Tuesday and now, on Thursday, a broad river straddled the best part of the lawn on the house side and the flower beds before the fence on the far side. It flowed smoothly, unlike the churnings and bubblings of previous days, as if bloated and lazy after a heavy lunch. Stream-side rocks and grassy humps no longer interfered with its course; it slid right over them. A few watery swells and spirals were the only signs that they were there. Rain pockmarked the surface in its steady, heavy fall, and the surface constantly smoothed itself out, only to be battered down again and again. She imagined a battle between the two - Elves hurling raindrop after raindrop from the sky, and Water-Dwarves rebuilding their water-walls as fast as they were broken. Every so often the wind gusted and whiplashed raindrops across the water and sent surface shivers against the current.

Her dad had said that God had made the world in a week, and she wondered how long it would take him to flood it. Her dad had said that long ago God had been so upset with people that he had drowned the world and everyone in it, and had saved just two of every creature on Noah's boat. She had wondered how Noah and his wife had fed them all, and why the animals hadn't eaten each other, and why God had saved the snakes. St Patrick had driven all the snakes out of Ireland. She thought God was cruel to have drowned so many people. They couldn't all have been bad, even all the children and babies. Her dad had said that they were. He said God wanted to wash away Sin so that the world could be made a better place. He said that God would do it again if people carried on the way they were going.

She could see the start of the lane beyond the short gravel driveway beginning its flat winding way to the main road, three-quarters of a mile from the house. It was waterlogged, with only the verges and the grass-tufted centre poking out above the water, which had made two canals of the mud-brown ruts in between. The wet grass looked so much darker than it did in the sun. The lane was hedged with bramble and hawthorn, and she could remember Bramble Scrambles with her mum in the early evenings of late summers when the sun was turning orange. The first time, she had shocked herself in the hall mirror with her stained lips, and kept finding thorns and spiny needles and clinging burrs in her clothes. Once, she had tried to colour her lips by smearing blackberries across them. The juice got itself on her nose, and ran down her chin in streaks.

She left the window and sat on her bed, waking up Pooh and Piglet who had been snoring away oblivious of the dismal afternoon. Pooh was lazy by nature, and Piglet was too nervous to do anything much by himself. She lifted them up and they hugged each other, and then they both hugged her. Pooh went to sit by himself on another part of the bed and began to make up a hum, so she took Piglet between her feet and lay back with her legs in the air so that Piglet was suspended above her face, looking down. They began to talk about the Floods and how their friends might get on, and she said her school friends lived in towns and wouldn't mind all the rain very much, and Piglet said that Owl would be all right but what about Eyeore?, and they agreed that they might try a Rescue of some kind, if Pooh would help.

It was Carol from the village who brought her Pooh Bear and Piglet after her mum had gone. Carol said they needed love, and would take a lot of looking after. Pooh was yellow and Piglet was pink, but Pooh had a dark blue stain on his head by his left ear. He had a big nose and a smiley mouth. Piglet didn't have a mouth at all. He had little round eyes and always looked More than a Little Anxious. He needed more looking after than Pooh. They lived on her pillow, which was quite big enough for the three of them, and sometimes they got cold and burrowed down beneath the covers.

Carol used to come once a week for the dusting and the linen. She was immensely fat and smelled of liver and peppermints. She wore her streaked and greying hair in a loose bun, which was slightly squint and looked as though it was constantly trying to ease itself off her large head. Carol chatted to her like a best friend, and hugged her, and called her a Poppet. But she made her feel a bit uncomfortable. Sometimes Carol brought her crumpled paperback books with dirty, thumb-worn edges and the names of her children scribbled over the blank pages inside the front covers. Her dad had fallen out with Carol, and she didn't come anymore. The house was dustier now, especially upstairs.

Her dad had a bad leg and hardly ever left the ground floor. His bedroom was downstairs, next to the living room. At eight-o-clock each night, or a little after if his reading from the Bible had gone on longer than usual, she would kiss him in his chair, and then would go up to her room alone. The sheets on her bed were always cold. She would curl up like a hedgehog till she was warm, and then when she stretched her legs out the sheets around her feet would still be starchy and freezing.

They had a wood-burning stove in the cellar, and when it was lit the heat would rise through the whole house. She would watch the wood crackling, and pretend it was the wicked witch from Hansel and Gretel. But her dad often kept an open fire in the living room instead, and that meant the top of the house was usually chilly. Carol said she thought her dad forgot about her up there. 'Don't let him forget about you, Poppet!' she said.

Besides the wood-stove, they had their own small generator, which her dad had built. He was good at fixing things, but he couldn't do much now because of his leg. He used to repair the inside of the house while she and her mum did the garden. He had once retiled the bathroom, and when her mum had told her he was inside 'grouting', she thought he was in a bad mood. She had held a measuring tape for him once, and he had shown her how to use a 'spirit-level'. She had thought it was something he had borrowed from the church. Her mum used to say he spent more time fixing the house than living in it. There were no power cables running to the house, no water-pipes as they had their own supply, and no phone lines. Her dad didn't like telephones, nor televisions, nor computers. He said that the only thing that connected them to the world at large was the track running to the main road, and that that was how he liked things. Her dad was home most of the time, or he was out at the church. He hadn't worked since she could remember. He read a lot, though. He kept an evenly stacked column of books on the table by his chair in the living room. One of the books at the bottom of the pile was called Wide Sargasso Sea, and had a blue spine. He had put to memory whole chapters of the Bible.

Pooh was proving a reluctant rescuer. He said he didn't have the right type of fur for rain, as it sucked it in rather than pushed it out and, besides, having some Experience of being a cloud for a short time, he thought that clouds didn't really get on with bears. She said she had seen her mum's face in a cloud once, but it had turned into a crouching rabbit with a bobtail. Her dad never really said where mum went, but he said that sometimes God wanted the better people upstairs with him.

There were no pictures of her mum in the house, except for the one in her dad's bedroom. It was locked-up in a drawer. She had found it when he was out. She had prised open the heavy door and teetered into the room on arched feet, pretending the swirls of the carpet pattern were stepping stones. Sitting at the huge dusty walnut desk she had pretended to be a servant to the king, writing out his regal decrees. Unable to find a Particular Document which was critical to the life of a condemned slave, she had begun to rifle through the desk drawers. The higher drawers contained papers, mostly old and curled at the edges. Lower down, the drawers were filled with letters, opened but still in their envelopes, various paperweights of different sizes, numerous pairs of glasses in velvet or leather cases, a small torch and a cracked magnifying glass, and several satiny cloth rectangles printed with 'His Master's Voice' in the centre in gold under a picture of a little dog sitting by a big horn. The lowest drawer on the left side of the desk was the only one that was locked, but the key was left in it, and inside, on top of a small bundle of letters, she found her mother, less pretty than she remembered, but younger than she had ever seen her and smiling. She had kind eyes. She went back whenever her dad was out, but after that first time the drawer was always locked and the key was never there.

His voice was calling her. Tea-time. She put Pooh carefully back in his place on the pillow, kissing his nose. She straightened out her yellow frock, pulled the curtains across the window to keep out Wandering Trolls, and went downstairs. Out of the landing window she saw rainwater funnelling from a hole in the gutter of the flat garage roof. Yesterday she had seen water bubbling out from under the garage door. The hall at the bottom of the stairs had a full length mirror on the wall which made it look bigger, but it was narrow and always smelled musty, and if she went down with bare feet the carpet felt slightly damp. Now, in the early evening, the hall was dim. Rain made the light fall blue, heavy and drear. She walked to the far end where stronger light filtered under the kitchen door. A faint warmth brushed her cheek as she opened the door a crack and squeezed through. Her dad was sitting in his place at the table, and as she pushed the door to again he told her that Procrastination was the thief of time. She pulled out her chair, which was heavy and creaked and screeched over the uneven flags. The table was set with two glass bowls in the centre with long blue plastic serving forks. One contained quartered tomatoes, the other chopped lettuce and peppers glistening with olive oil. Her plate had on it two slices of unbuttered wholemeal bread. Her dad didn't eat meat, and he didn't eat butter or margarine. Her mum used to give her drop-scones spread with thick butter, which had come out of a silver package with a three-petalled green flower on top and the words 'Product of Irish Dairies'. It was kept on the top shelf of the fridge door next to the eggs.

After grace, she took some lettuce, carefully avoiding the cubes of pepper, and two segments of tomato. Her dad told her that she needed more, so she took another two pieces of tomato; but some juice from the second piece dripped as she balanced it towards her plate. Her dad went for a cloth and told her that it was very important to move the plate near to the bowl or the bowl near to the plate. Now he would have to wash the table-cloth. She ate the tomatoes first and then the lettuce layered on the bread. The clock in the kitchen had a loud, lazy tick and the rain outside could be heard, falling heavily. There was a kind of layered rhythm. Something in her dad's jaw made a dull clicking as he chewed, and sometimes she paused her own chewing to listen. When he had finished, her dad told her that the church roof had sprung a leak.

'Mrs Holland says that not a few of the prayer books are ruined. I can't pretend I'm surprised. They should have had it looked at before now. It's the old story, the grasshopper who sang all summer.'

Her dad had told her that God lived in the church. If he did he would be very miserable and cold. She thought he lived in the sky. Her mum had said that God lived in her and in all the people in the world.

Mrs Holland did the flowers at the church. She was very old and had curly white hair, and wore big glasses, and spoke funny. She sometimes gave her throat pastilles which were very strong and made her cough. She had once asked Mrs Holland what Holland was like, and Mrs Holland had said it was very flat and had walls round it to keep the water out, and people rode bicycles. Her dad told her later that Mrs Holland was Scottish and had never been Abroad.

When her dad rose to do the washing-up, she slid off her chair and left the kitchen. In the hallway she walked towards herself in the mirror at the foot of the stairs, and saw that she had olive oil stains on her yellow dress. She spat on her fingers and tried to wipe them off. She stood still for a time pretending to be Alice. She looked behind her once or twice to see if everything was exactly the same as it appeared in the mirror. She reached out and put a finger to the glass, hoping it might pass through. At this moment she saw her dad in the mirror coming out of the kitchen. He told her that Vanity was a sin and would lead to Worse, and then he went into the living room.

She went up the stairs, pretending they were steeper than they were, and that they made her fall backwards after every few steps. She lay on her bed looking for several minutes at the mottled patterns of plaster on her ceiling. Then she sat up and pulled Pooh and Piglet onto her lap, and bounced them up and down, one on each knee. Pooh looked somehow despondent. His eyes seemed to bulge more than usual, and his smile seemed a little turned down at the corners. She was necessarily severe with him.

'Eyeore is expected to be sorry for himself. Not you. Can't you try to make another song, or a hum, or something?'

She tried to do it for him, but couldn't get past the first two lines, which might equally well have been the last two. She went to the window. God was still crying, and the clouds were as dark and thick as ever. The swollen stream had edged a little further up the lawn. She climbed onto the bed and played at being Piglet Entirely Surrounded by Water.

# Cold Snap

A sudden ice-cap seems to slide
along the glittered dancing floor,
like clouds across the sky outside
that cover up the stars.

The dancers stop, as if to hear
a wind they never heard before,
hustling down the chimney shafts,
buffeting the restaurant door.

They huddle from the cold snap;
their dinner-jackets feel too thin.
It stills their half-mad gaiety
to a gallery of grins.

The shutter clacks. The ice-cap
shivers back across the room
but the glitter's lost its lustre
and the band sounds out of tune.

It leaves five men in black and white,
awkward with each other now.
A frieze of snow and shadow.
The party is undone.

# Building Alluvium

Fifth gear and coasting in the mindless flow
of traffic, following the monotony
of engine throb, wet tarmac and white line,
I cross the road-bridge.
I see, glancing right, the sloped mud-flats
of the widening estuary,
silk-smooth, storm-dark, and glistening.
Sandy wastes of stink and slime.

*Alluvium.*
The word whispers languid grace.
Perhaps that's why I still remember
this flotsam
from school geography.
*Alluvium.*
Diverse matter, disintegrated bits of things, carried,
then deposited,
by river-flows or floods.

It might also be a distant country.
The Alluvian hinterland.
Alluvian fields.
An Alluvian utopia.

As a kid, I'd take up dried drift-reeds
as fishing rods.

*This is alluvium, spooling through my mind now.*
*This is restful resignation to the fancy of currents...*
*This is casting off and drifting...*
*This is suspended animation in clear, cool water...*
*This is lazy pirouettes in eddies, and twirlings through deep pools...*

Sudden sun, shaken free of heavy clouds,
dazzles over the slippery flats and strikes my eyes,
bleaching everything.
A blink reveals all that solar energy gathered
in one moment of electro-plated glory.
Land is cased in a chrome shell.
Molten metal has quickly cooled to solid cast
over sediment slopes.
The deep vein of the river still moves, but slow, like mercury.

In the river's quiet silver, I'm almost letting go, almost
floating, and the car is drifting right.
I jerk back, correcting my course.
Hard tarmac lies ahead,
but a deposit has been laid.
I will add this crossing to my mounting banks of silt.
Slowly, I am building a country.